SOCIETAL COHESION
AND
THE GLOBALISING
ECONOMY

WHAT DOES THE FUTURE HOLD?

ORGANISATION FOR ECONOMIC CO-OPERATION AND DEVELOPMENT

ORGANISATION FOR ECONOMIC CO-OPERATION AND DEVELOPMENT

Pursuant to Article 1 of the Convention signed in Paris on 14th December 1960, and which came into force on 30th September 1961, the Organisation for Economic Co-operation and Development (OECD) shall promote policies designed:

- to achieve the highest sustainable economic growth and employment and a rising standard of living in Member countries, while maintaining financial stability, and thus to contribute to the development of the world economy;
- to contribute to sound economic expansion in Member as well as non-member countries in the process of economic development; and
- to contribute to the expansion of world trade on a multilateral, non-discriminatory basis in accordance with international obligations.

The original Member countries of the OECD are Austria, Belgium, Canada, Denmark, France, Germany, Greece, Iceland, Ireland, Italy, Luxembourg, the Netherlands, Norway, Portugal, Spain, Sweden, Switzerland, Turkey, the United Kingdom and the United States. The following countries became Members subsequently through accession at the dates indicated hereafter: Japan (28th April 1964), Finland (28th January 1969), Australia (7th June 1971), New Zealand (29th May 1973), Mexico (18th May 1994), the Czech Republic (21st December 1995), Hungary (7th May 1996), Poland (22nd November 1996) and the Republic of Korea (12th December 1996). The Commission of the European Communities takes part in the work of the OECD (Article 13 of the OECD Convention).

Publié en français sous le titre :

COHÉSION SOCIALE ET MONDIALISATION DE L'ÉCONOMIE
Ce que l'avenir nous réserve

FOREWORD

For over a decade, OECD countries have been committed to a cluster of economic policies aimed at encouraging macroeconomic stabilization, structural adjustment and the globalisation of production and distribution. Although these policies have been generally successful in supporting economic growth, combating inflation and reducing current-account imbalances, there is now pressure on many governments to take stock of the longer-term societal implications that are beginning to emerge. In part this is because of a growing political disenchantment arising from the increasing income polarisation, persistently high levels of unemployment, and widespread social exclusion that are manifesting themselves in varying ways across North America, Europe and OECD Pacific. The diffusion of this malaise throughout society threatens to undermine both the drive towards greater economic flexibility and the policies that encourage strong competition, globalisation and technological innovation.

With these concerns in mind, the OECD organised a Forum for the Future conference in December 1996. Its primary objective was to stimulate innovative thinking about ways to maintain future societal cohesion in the face of a dynamic economy that thrives on a high degree of flexibility. One of the main questions to be explored from the broad perspective of societal cohesion was, what kind of society and social systems will be able to cope with the exigencies of greater economic flexibility? How much and what kinds of adaptability will be required of individuals, firms, political parties, public administrations, voluntary organisations and other collective institutions?

The discussion during the one-day conference was divided into two parts. The first session dealt with the long-run implications of current economic and social policies. The second examined alternative scenarios for societal cohesion in the future. The meeting was chaired by Donald J. Johnston, Secretary-General of the OECD, and participants around the table were drawn from the highest ranks of government, business and the academic world.

This publication brings together the papers presented at the meeting as well as an introductory contribution and summary of the main points of the discussions prepared by the Secretariat. The book is published on the responsibility of the Secretary-General of the OECD.

TABLE OF CONTENTS

ECONOMIC FLEXIBILITY AND SOCIETAL COHESION IN THE TWENTY-FIRST CENTURY: AN OVERVIEW OF THE ISSUES AND KEY POINTS OF THE DISCUSSION

by

Wolfgang Michalski, Riel Miller and Barrie Stevens
OECD Secretariat, Advisory Unit to the Secretary-General

Turbulence – economic, social, technological – is a long-standing attribute of human society, as is the capacity to survive it. Indeed, the century now drawing to a close provides ample evidence of how people can adapt and even thrive in a world of rapid and pervasive change. However, profound and unanticipated transformations are not a virtue *per se*. Nor are tests of human adaptability. Rather, it is safe to assume that most people prefer a world where life is characterised by stability, continuity, predictability, and secure access to material well-being.

Societies with these attributes garner more easily the commitment and adherence that sustain societal cohesion over time. Yet, many of the economic policies pursued for some years now by OECD Member countries encourage the productive turmoil of relentlessly competitive markets – a constant process of creation and destruction that politicians and electorates seem to have almost universally embraced, showing a strong willingness to forgo tranquillity for the sake of greater prosperity. At the same time, there are signs of growing strains on the fabric of OECD societies, in the form of stubbornly high levels of unemployment, widening income disparities, persistent poverty, and social exclusion.

Of course, competition and structural change are not fundamentally incompatible with societal cohesion. On the contrary, they are a motor of the economic growth and prosperity on which cohesion can thrive. Reciprocally, a strong social fabric provides a secure basis for the flexibility and risk-taking which are the life-blood of vibrant economic activity and wealth creation. Striking a sustainable balance between dynamism and security constitutes one of the primary missions of the political processes. The capacity to find the appropriate balance, thereby avoiding both stagnation and social fragmentation, is one of the key strengths of OECD democracies – a strength that will probably be put to the test over the next two decades.

LONG-RUN IMPLICATIONS OF CURRENT ECONOMIC AND SOCIAL POLICIES

Since the early 1980s, OECD Member countries have pursued a basically similar set of economic policies, including: macroeconomic policies that target low inflation and sound fiscal balances; structural adjustment measures aimed at improving the functioning of product, capital and labour markets; and the liberalisation of trade, investment and technology flows to enhance global economic efficiency. These policies are considered to have contributed to bringing about a number of significant improvements. Inflation in most of the OECD area has fallen sharply from its peak in 1980, when consumer prices increased by over 13 per cent, to its current level of 2-3 per cent. The deterioration in cyclically adjusted government balances (*i.e.* structural budget deficits) observed throughout the OECD area in the late 1980s/early 1990s has been reversed or halted in almost all cases. Regulatory reform and privatisation, prominent features of the US economy in the late 1970s/early 1980s, spread in varying intensities to parts of Europe and OECD Pacific, and international trade benefited significantly from a lowering of import tariffs.

At the same time, however, there is a strong sense of worsening social circumstances for large segments of OECD populations. Continental Europe now lives with double-digit unemployment rates and increasing concerns that many individuals are being marginalised from mainstream economic life. In the United States, average wage growth has been slow (indeed, negative for less-skilled workers), inequality has been rising, and poverty has been growing both in general and especially among children. Income inequality and poverty have also increased in Australia and the United Kingdom. And in Japan, unemployment – official and disguised – is mounting. Problems of social exclusion and a growing sense of insecurity are manifest in virtually all OECD countries. Governments almost everywhere are conscious of the risks to society's cohesiveness; yet, the indications are that they may hold the current economic policy course for many years to come.

The longer-term economic outlook

Awareness of the benefits of general price stability and predictability has become increasingly entrenched, not only among policy-makers but also in the business community and society at large. Not surprisingly, therefore, most long-term projections by independent research institutions expect consumer price increases in the OECD area to remain around the 2-3 per cent range over the coming years. The pincer effect of demographic pressures will continue to build up in many OECD countries through the next decades as demands on government welfare spending rise and declining labour force growth reduces the capacity to finance it. Controlling and reducing general public debt – already averaging three-quarters of OECD GDP – and, over the medium term at least, movement towards European monetary union will provide additional impulses for fiscal consolidation in the future. In addition, the expectation of sectoral and economy-wide efficiency gains from privatisation will encourage further sales of public assets in Continental Europe (where it is thought that the equivalent of some $250 billion of state-owned assets remain to be sold off), and also in Japan.

Moreover, with the Uruguay Round agreement in place, tariff barriers and some non-tariff barriers are set to fall further, and new rules of the game are emerging for trade in services and the international protection of property rights. Consequently, international trade is expected to expand by around 6.5 per cent per annum over the next ten years. Similarly, barriers to international flows of direct investment will diminish substantially as international agreements, such as the Multilateral Agreement on Investment currently under negotiation at OECD, fall into place.

The chapters prepared for this publication highlight the wide range of economic outcomes that are possible. OECD economies may, for example, find themselves on a much faster growth trajectory twenty years hence if productivity payoffs from the diffusion of new technologies, market liberalisation and globalisation come on stream. Alternatively, productivity growth may slow even more abruptly than anticipated, fiscal consolidation may become even more intractable, and international trade and investment may come to be widely perceived as exacerbating disruption and dislocation, unleashing protectionist and potentially recessionary forces. Or, at least in the medium term – and this is perhaps the most likely scenario – OECD countries may continue to muddle through, with slow but positive productivity and economic growth, virtually no labour force growth, and incomes rising only slowly.

Clearly, different economic outcomes will trigger different social outcomes. A "no change" scenario might hold some prospect of improvement in incomes across the OECD area, but other aspects remain disquieting nonetheless. The plight of the poorest Americans could well deepen, unemployment in Europe might become even more entrenched (with considerably less income support from welfare), and Japan could find existing traditional institutions (such as lifelong employment and the seniority principle) under mounting pressure. By contrast, in a high-growth world driven by gains from technological innovation, market liberalisation and internationalisation, the much-improved economic climate would create more room for manoeuvre on the social front. The United States could see declining poverty rates and improved earnings even for the less skilled; European governments would have much more scope for strengthening the social safety net thanks to higher employment, increased tax returns and healthier fiscal positions; and Japan would be put on a stronger footing to face its problem of a rapidly ageing society. And finally, in a recessionary scenario, the social situation of many OECD citizens would clearly deteriorate.

Despite the strong likelihood of the current set of economic policies continuing into the next century, there remains the question of whether there are viable alternative economic policy approaches, and whether such alternative approaches would lead to more favourable social outcomes without being detrimental to economic performance.

Proponents of alternative economic policy approaches fall into three broad (and admittedly very stylised) categories. There are those who believe that the inflation mentality of the past has been conquered and that the monetary authorities can now afford to be less restrictive with respect to the money supply. Increased activity, it is contended, would translate into real growth and not inflation, because the highly competitive global economy would restrain the pricing power of companies, thus ensuring they would raise profitability by boosting efficiency. The result would be to lift OECD economies onto a higher growth plane, potentially reducing unemployment, poverty, etc. Critics argue that in at least two of the major economies, the United States and Japan, official unemployment is already low; inflationary pressures would be inevitable, not least because looser monetary policy would lead to a weaker currency in what is an increasingly open world economy.

In the opposite camp are those who would prefer to limit disruption in the domestic economy by slowing down the requisite adaptation to global competition and technological change. The risk is not only that protectionist sentiment would gain ground, but also that structural adjustment would be merely postponed, thus prolonging painful social readjustments. A third camp proposes a judicious mix of monetary and fiscal policy, coupled with even faster liberalisation, deregulation and privatisation than experienced at present, to ensure speedy adjustment to a rapidly evolving globalised economy. Yet here the problem comes full circle, for the risk is of even higher transition costs and thus an even greater threat of social backlash against the economic policies in place.

Challenges to societal cohesion

In a world characterised by globalisation and rapid technological progress, nowhere will change be felt more acutely than in the market-place and at work. Looking at the next twenty years, two interrelated trends are likely to propel OECD countries towards ever-greater degrees of economic flexibility: with labour, goods and services markets exposed to deregulation, globalisation and technological change, there may be greater volatility and pliability in response to a full range of intense competitive pressures; and in many branches of the economy, production processes and the firms that oversee them are likely to be reorganised, becoming less hierarchical and more open to change and innovation.

Barring a collapse of the trend towards pro-market reforms at the national, regional and global levels, a cluster of developments will probably be at the fore-front of market expansion and the intensification of competition over the next couple of decades. First, there is likely to be an important expansion of the geo-graphical scope of market relationships and the number of people connected to a wider range of markets. Second, the diversity of products (goods and services, tangible and intangible) available across this broader range of markets will probably continue to grow as the variety of suppliers and the technology of production offer greater selection. Third, the swiftly emerging global information infrastructure will greatly facilitate access to economic information such as prices and product and service availability (intermediate inputs as well as final consumer items). Fourth, international agreements along with improvements in transportation technology and logistical co-ordination will also facilitate the delivery of goods and services, particularly digital commodities supplied over electronic networks such as the Internet. Fifth, policies aimed at privatisation, deregulation and safeguarding against excess concentration or collusion will help to expand the scope and com-petitiveness of markets. Lastly – and largely because of greater geographic cover-age, output diversity, fast access and ease of delivery – it seems reasonable to expect that markets will touch more aspects of daily life.

In a nutshell, markets and competition will become more important, and with them an expanding range of opportunities for economic growth and prosperity. However, responding to these opportunities will require considerable organisa-tional changes in the workplace, some of which are already under way. A rich if at times bewildering array of new management theories and practices points towards a trend break away from the traditional top-down command-and-control systems of mass-production industries. These changes may lead to much greater decentralisa-tion of decision-making responsibility. A significant segment of the workforce may become independent entrepreneurs as networks become more transparent and consumers shift roles from the demand to the supply side by adding significantly more value (conception) directly into the production process. Much will depend on the capacity of information technology and institutional systems that manage risk to support an economy where knowledge is highly dispersed and exchanged at almost no cost. Should this come to pass, working life could lose many of its current spatial, temporal and organisational patterns, and be replaced by a more autonomous, innovation-intensive process. Just-in-time production of just-invented products will require highly efficient information, demand and supply networks.

Market-related and organisational changes on this scale could also alter a range of familiar practices and institutions which serve to reassure investors. Many economic agents may face higher risk profiles in an economy dominated by less hierarchical production processes and quickly shifting worldwide competition. Adapting to tomorrow's highly contingent, flexible economy may entail changes to many of the traditional bulwarks of societal cohesion. Familiar patterns and institutions that helped manage risk and provided medium-term predictability, such as trade unions, professional organisations, income support and educational systems, might be hard-pressed – in current forms – to dampen the inherent turbulence of such decentralised, spontaneous markets and methods of production. In some areas, there are signs that alternatives may be emerging – for example, the growing use of market-based insurance instruments and the spread of voluntary associations – but in others the vacuum has yet to be filled.

Outside the world of work, in the household and daily life, the story may not be much different. A number of demographic and social trends can be expected to put pressure on the social fabric of most OECD countries in the coming years. Primary among these is the ageing of the population, with its potential for inter-generational conflicts over income transfers and the pace of socio-economic change. It is conceivable that the large elderly contingents of the next century, better organised and more prone to participate in political processes, will attempt to impose their values and interests on younger generations. A second related source of societal tension has already appeared and looks set to intensify as strong public demand (pensions, health care, education) and greater diversity of need (heterogeneous family types, women in the labour market, immigrants, youth) confront limited tax revenue, making it difficult on both fiscal and efficiency grounds to sustain centralised, universalistic-type social programmes. This will also complicate the task of countering the unease and anxiety that are stirred up by various forms of protracted social exclusion.

All of these risks are compounded by another challenge to societal cohesion stemming from the need to reconcile women's reproductive and economic roles in ways that are equitable and efficient. Here again, the underlying social and economic structures have shifted in ways that put pressure on established institutional frameworks. For instance, high rates of female labour force participation, reflecting the need and desire for income and independence, call for changes in the provision of essential household services like child care. Similarly, restoring that portion of the social fabric undermined by growing child-poverty will need to take into account the reality of women's generally lower income levels and preponderance as the head of household in single-parent families. Lastly, there is the trend towards greater cultural diversity. As technology, migration and trade all shrink the practical distances separating people, there is perforce a greater likelihood of rubbing elbows. The reclaiming of local or historical cultural identities along with the vital voices of immigrants, all within a more tolerant legal framework (granting human rights to many formerly denied the privilege), could make cleavages previously papered over or suppressed much more apparent. The reality – in certain cases, semblance – of a homogeneous national identity once so central to societal cohesion may give way to a fragmentation of cultural aspirations and values.

The responses of OECD countries to these varied challenges will evolve out of the existing robust and fairly flexible institutional and social bases. Many innovative and successful adaptations are already taking place. But two questions are worth posing at this point. First, will the pervasive and cumulative impact of economic, social and technological changes demand responses that depart significantly from current approaches to assuring societal cohesion? And second, how can new solutions to the challenge of forging a cohesive society effectively take into account the distinctive values and political choices that characterise the diversity of OECD countries? The following sections take some initial steps towards answering these complex and important questions.

PATHS TO SOCIETAL COHESION IN THE FUTURE: DEVELOPING ALTERNATIVE SCENARIOS

Societal cohesion is the outcome of a complex blend of factors that change from one country to another and over time. One of the primary or at least most readily identifiable sources of societal cohesion is the state. This perception has arisen naturally over the last century as the government's role in social protection and services, from pensions and welfare payments to schooling and health care, has been the glue holding many aspects of society together. Major contributor to a long period of rapid growth and rising standards of living in OECD countries, the welfare state in its many different forms is seen to be central to providing citizens with a sense of security and reason to be committed to the society in which they live.

Recently, however, the positive role of the welfare state has been called into question. For some the commitments to full employment, public-sector industries, labour market regulation, public services protected from market forces, and income security that blunt incentives to work and save are responsible for many current economic and social difficulties. For others the realities of fiscal limits, high unemployment, changing family structures and the stress of poverty on the social fabric also call for a new approach to social protection. Although the welfare state is coping better in some countries than in others, reform of social policy is high on the public agenda across the OECD area.

Seen from an international perspective, there are important differences across OECD countries in the concerns and aspirations that are likely to play a central role in arriving at the much-sought-after balance between economic flexibility and societal cohesion: American worries about growing income cleavages and a shrinking middle class are pitted against a reluctance to lose a leading edge in economic dynamism; Japanese attachment to a tightly cohesive society versus pressures to reduce economic rigidities and to facilitate greater heterogeneity; and European desires to safeguard wide-ranging welfare entitlements against the search for stronger work incentives, less expensive low-skilled labour and the generally more responsive economy capable of reducing high levels of unemployment.

Many options for improving the functioning of the welfare state are under consideration or already being implemented. In particular there is widespread recognition of the need to eliminate from income transfer programmes poverty traps and other disincentives to work and save. The aggressive pursuit of active labour market policies, lifelong learning and efficiency in public services has been accompanied by privatisation, programme redesign, management renewal, and tax and regulatory reforms. In many OECD countries there is a general recognition of the need to redirect social expenditure away from (some) relatively well-off elderly people towards supporting poorer families with children and enabling currently excluded people to become established in the labour market.

A range of innovative ideas – some of which are presented in the following chapters of this book – are up for discussion, including opt-out programmes, government loan guarantees, support accounts, and benefit transfer programmes. By shifting from a social expenditure to a social investment perspective, it is expected that considerable progress can be made in transforming the welfare state. Without losing sight of the important variations across OECD countries, implementation of these new approaches aims to provide a degree of security and social protection that encourages individuals to take risks and be flexible, without hindering job mobility or abandoning those facing long-term exclusion from the labour market.

Projecting such incremental changes to the welfare state into the future is one useful way of picturing how the mechanisms of societal cohesion might evolve in OECD countries over the coming decades. Another way of exploring many of the same issues, but less constrained by the initial starting point, is to develop broad-brush scenarios of how a hypothetical society might function around 2015. Such scenarios, although not necessarily corresponding to any specific future reality, have the virtue of exposing possible forms of social organisation or economic structure that are likely to fall outside the scope of more incremental and extrapolated approaches. Analysing alternative or contrasting scenarios also makes somewhat easier the difficult task of exposing the central role of values or political preferences – and the pivotal role of the political process – in forging a sustainable balance between economic flexibility and societal cohesion.

In the scenarios presented below, it is the assertion of distinctive cultural and political values that largely sets the parameters for the range of imaginable societal configurations. In the first, the "individualistic scenario", society does the utmost to encourage individual freedom and responsibility, allowing the verdict of unconstrained markets to provide the acute incentives associated with the prospect of great wealth or severe poverty. In the alternative "solidaristic scenario", much greater emphasis is put on collective organisations, universal rights and redistributive frameworks as ways of hedging risks and spurring the innovation markets demand.

By accepting at the outset the dynamism of a flexible economy, both scenarios come to share the challenges of but not the solutions to achieving societal cohesion. As noted above, future economic flexibility promises new, contingent and spontaneous forms of work and enterprise organisation. More competitive, knowledge-based, global and networked economies may alter the constraints of time and space (when and where people work and live) by producing less mass-based patterns. Coping with and overcoming the possible negative impacts of these trends is what the scenarios have in common. They diverge when it comes to identifying what might keep such a dynamic and potentially eclectic social system together. Operationally, the differences are mainly embedded in alternative institutional frameworks – the scale of the role accorded public (if not governmental) bodies and the extent to which universally applicable rules are established and implemented.

An individualistic scenario

Radically reducing the role of governments in all domains – social programmes, economic regulation, public enterprises – offers a fairly direct path to greater flexibility in the allocation of resources by individuals and firms. For individuals, the dismantling of publicly imposed programmes, services and standards could open the way to a wider range of choices for such things as pension schemes, educational institutions, telecommunications suppliers, electricity providers, and insurers against illness or lack of paid work. Enterprises, of whatever scale, are also liberated from many of the restraints imposed by public mandates: numerous social expenses, investment restrictions, product regulations, etc. In this scenario, economic agents – individuals and firms – achieve greater allocative efficiency because a massive reduction (not elimination) of collectively imposed public policies increases both the available choices and the direct responsibility for the choices made.

New social service options are encouraged by ending or significantly reducing public sector monopoly provision across industry and service sectors – from social insurance programmes such as pensions and unemployment benefits to health care, education and even some policing. Centrally imposed standards that restrict the scope of economic agents when it comes to process and product innovation are eliminated, relaxed or devolved to the local or regional level. Constraints on commerce – wherever, whenever and (in fully liberal fashion) however – are relaxed to a point far beyond today's standards. On the other hand, there is an extension of property rights and protection (particularly in the growing realm of intangible and digital output) in order to safeguard investment incentives and encourage the market along all potentially profitable avenues. Criminal law would remain one of the major constraints on individual freedom.

The greatest virtue of such an unbounded society is its capacity to reap the full rewards of market efficiency and individual choice. Transactions are not only unconstrained but able to penetrate further into all aspects of life and render the clear verdict of the market. Incentives to work, save, invest and consume are transparent and subject to unobstructed individual calculation. It is expected that many of the technical as opposed to state-imposed obstacles to market functioning, like the cost of accurate and timely information for making transaction choices, will be largely overcome by the emerging power of the global information infrastructure. Should this technological wave not only increase the efficiency of market functioning but also help pave the way for a long-run investment boom in the context of stable macroeconomic conditions, then this scenario could probably deliver the considerable prosperity needed to gain the widespread commitment upon which societal cohesion depends.

Robust rates of economic growth will be essential to the success of this individualistic model, for two reasons. First, in such a high-risk environment, almost all segments of society will need to be able to share the dream of eventually being a winner – a common, unifying belief in the chance of success that cushions the reality of extreme inequality. Secondly, the society will still need to be wealthy enough to attend to the minimum needs of the losers and those incapable of participating. If for some reason the productivity gains or macroeconomic stability do not pan out, this scenario's chance of sustaining social cohesion could rapidly unravel.

Finally, there are a series of endogenous impediments to the realisation of this scenario, two of which are worth mentioning here. First, many factors could slow down or block the penetration and greater efficiency of market relationships. The most important mitigating factor could prove to be the natural tendency towards market imperfection. Should competition policy frameworks and enforcement prove inadequate, the highly unequal distribution of economic power might be used to resist competition and slow the restructuring of existing organisations and markets. Or, it is possible that the powerful might be too severe in imposing flexibility upon the weak, with potentially serious repercussions for social unrest. In either case, the dynamism and prosperity crucial to the success of this scenario would be nipped in the bud.

A second endogenous obstacle emerges from the difficulty of developing collective frameworks. Here, the tension is between unfettered individualism and the sacrifice of certain freedoms for the sake of creating mutually beneficial agreements regarding, for instance, income redistribution, environmental standards, consumer protection and punishment for criminal activity. In an individualistic society it may be difficult (very costly or protracted) to establish some of the basic rules of the game that are so essential for the trust and confidence without which markets cannot function efficiently. Indeed, the combination of unlimited accumulation of wealth (market power) and weak collective institutions could usher in the worst of both worlds: uncompetitive monopoly or collusive behaviour in the market-place and risk-adverse defensive behaviour among individuals.

Solidaristic scenario

Societal cohesion in this second scenario depends heavily on strong collective – particularly public – institutions and shared values. Unlike the individualistic approach of the previous scenario, in this social configuration rapid innovation and adaptability are supported by public institutions that diversify risk, service collective needs (market and non-market) and significantly intensify participatory democracy. Flexibility is delivered by altering the scale and relationship between individuals and their community. Faceless, distant, unresponsive bureaucracies are replaced by local and familiar organisations where individuals are obliged, as the quid pro quo of being a member of the community, to participate directly.

In return, citizens are offered a range of resources and services useful for production and consumption, such as learning, health care, technology diffusion, risk insurance of various kinds and sound environmental conditions. Local well-being, that embraces and partially merges elements such as medical care, education and welfare programmes into the overarching notion of a "healthy community", becomes the responsibility of the people who live in the community. As a result there is a substantial improvement in the incentives and quality of information available for making efficient decisions, to the point where collectively provided infrastructure is no longer a constraint on social and economic flexibility. Instead, people are liberated in their approach to learning, working and taking risks in the worldwide knowledge economy.

Here again, the productivity-enhancing impact of the global information infrastructure plays a critical enabling role. Emboldened by easy access to consumer demand from around the planet, by the creative resources made available by information technology and by the support of a healthy community, producers will turn the old slogan on its head by thinking locally and acting globally. This is, however, contingent on three additional important attributes of a solidaristic scenario. First, it must be possible to establish a redistributive framework nationally and/or regionally to ensure that successful, healthy communities can assist less fortunate or dysfunctional communities. One version of such a redistributive framework might be a universal basic income within a nation or region, whereby income transfer is not linked to individual employment-related circumstances but solely to the individual's citizenship status. Specific economic rights are established that all citizens grant each other as a component of their citizenship. To help overcome the risk of thereby cementing permanent exclusion from the production process, entitlement is dependent on a minimum age of the recipient and is accompanied by measures that encourage rotation between gainful employment and other activities outside the labour market.

A second condition for success of the solidaristic model is the efficiency with which citizens participate in their community. Major strides could occur if power-sharing decentralisation were to combine with broadly diffused and effective information technologies to produce clearer signals and sound incentives regarding the individual choices that directly influence living and working conditions. Thirdly, a full transition from the uniformity of mass-production, mass-consumption society will require a reawakening of lost skills, tastes and distinctive culture. In a solidaristic social order, communities will be encouraged to nurture either a deepening of one particular culture or the mixing of many, thereby developing the knowledge content that will likely prove the vital factor behind productive success.

Risks abound, however. Foremost among the drawbacks of this solidaristic scenario is the danger of tyranny and/or inflexibility – not imposed by the economically powerful as in the individualist scenario, but by the collective values established in order to define effective communities. Building up frameworks capable of sustaining solidarity without compromising flexibility will be a daunting challenge. Intolerance and inequality among the multiplicity of self-identified communities may pose a serious threat to universal income schemes, peaceful coexistence and openness to competitive labour, financial, goods and services markets. Stagnation and lack of innovation could prevail should collective institutions end up obstructing clear market signals and flexible responses to competitive pressures. Finally, the efforts of a solidaristic society to encourage more efficient collective services through direct participation and continuous learning may come into conflict with efforts to forge the common views and values that are often seen as what makes a community worthy of individuals' commitment. Tolerance of other people's ideas and ways of looking at the world, one of the prerequisites for innovation and change, could turn out to be the enemy of the social homogeneity (or sameness of values) upon which solidarity depends.

These scenarios underscore the wide range of possible outcomes for OECD societies in the coming years. The actual contours of future societies will be shaped, in part, by values as determined by history, institutions and culture, and expressed through political choices. The question remains, however, whether there will be convergence or divergence in approaches to striking a sustainable balance between economic flexibility and societal cohesion. Pluralism in the balance ultimately struck could well test the compatibility of socio-economic systems in a world of closer global trade and investment links and growing international interdependence in general.

FINDING THE BALANCE BETWEEN ECONOMIC FLEXIBILITY AND SOCIETAL COHESION: A CHALLENGE FOR THE POLITICAL PROCESS

Conference participants identified a series of potentially major long-term challenges to societal cohesion arising from broad economic, technological, organisational and public sector trends. Their wide-ranging assessment of economic and social prospects set the stage for a multifaceted discussion of how to promote the sense of belonging, trust and security that are central to societal cohesion. The analysis converged on the need for innovative thinking about ways to counter social fragmentation and provide effective insurance against pertinent economic and social risks while encouraging community involvement and a sharing of aspirations and values. Overall, the long-run compatibility of economic flexibility with sustainable societal cohesion in OECD countries was viewed as likely to demand significant adaptation and innovation by governments, businesses and individual citizens.

Long-term challenges to societal cohesion in OECD countries

Conference participants agreed that pressures on societal cohesion are expected to evolve over the next two decades, as unemployment, earnings inequality, demographic shifts, technological progress, open trade and greater competition in less constrained market-places continue to contribute to economic and social turbulence. There was little doubt that major technological and organisational changes, many of which are already under way, are generally expected to sweep through all OECD economies, creating and demanding new approaches to risk management and encouraging social commitment. They also concurred that at the same time, demographic pressures induced by ageing and more diverse population structures will combine with stringent fiscal realities to push many OECD countries to rethink traditional public sector bulwarks of societal cohesion such as pension schemes, labour market programmes, and health and education policies.

With this vision of long-term challenges in mind, conference participants pointed out that the distribution of the costs and benefits of change will also pose a significant challenge. One view, argued strongly during the discussion, is that future societal cohesion will be unattainable politically and operationally if the sacrifices and transition costs demanded by a flexible economy are seen to fall only on the poorest and weakest segments of society, rather than on society as a whole.

Prospects for long-term economic growth, and policy

Many of the same forces that might unsettle societal cohesion were also deemed likely to play a preponderant role in shaping future growth trajectories. Population ageing and the shrinking of the active labour force could constrain growth in many OECD countries. Continuing technological developments with potentially dramatic productivity payoffs, possibly even in the service sector, were seen by some as an ongoing source of growth, even if low-skill workers may be further disadvantaged and income inequality heightened. With continuing liberalisation of trade and investment, globalisation is also expected to spur economic growth by encouraging international capital flows, advances in information, communication and transportation technologies, and a continued shift on the part of developing nations towards higher value-added activity.

On the policy side, conference participants expect Member countries to continue over the long term with the current mix of stringent monetary policy, fiscal restraint and an increased reliance on market forces. The long-run implications of this economic policy course were generally viewed as positive and superior to available alternatives. No gain and potentially considerable damage to growth prospects might be wrought by moves towards stimulatory fiscal policies that risk exacerbating public sector debt and reawakening inflation. Even more deleterious consequences were anticipated should there be sharp reversals of current policies towards more open trade and less restrained markets. Indeed, there was widespread agreement that policies promoting domestic and international competition will have a positive impact on growth by accelerating the introduction and diffusion of productivity-enhancing innovation.

Participants' assessments of the long-run economic growth outcomes, as shaped by the most plausible trends in the economic forces and policies, converged on a narrow range of possibilities. The scenario deemed most probable at the conference (dubbed the "doldrums scenario") envisages positive but low rates of economic growth over the next two decades. In the medium term there is a good chance of a pick-up in economic activity in Europe, structural reforms paying off in Japan and dynamism continuing in North America. Slow and steady economic growth is expected to contribute to long-run prospects for modest wage gains, quiescent inflation and stable or falling unemployment. Some conference participants did identify a number of negative factors that might slow economic growth further than generally anticipated. These include a failure of the productivity pay-off from investments in information technology and an ongoing drag exerted by slower efficiency gains in the service sectors. Other participants were more optimistic regarding the possibility of a technology take-off, particularly as younger and more computer-wise generations enter the labour force.

Adapting to change-driven growth

Conference participants generally agreed that the wide range of challenges to societal cohesion in OECD countries are unlikely to be resolved by the dividends arising from modest economic growth. Many of the anticipated difficulties in sustaining societal cohesion are not even due to economic growth *per se*, but rather stem from the profound nature of the demographic, economic and social changes that are expected to underlie any expansion. There was a generally shared view that unlike the past's familiar pattern of "productivity catch-up" and growth-driven change as higher income and investment alters the economic and social landscape, tomorrow's dynamic economy will evolve and grow in so far as it is capable of embracing the flexibility demanded by intensified competition and innovation.

The discussion stressed a number of factors likely simultaneously to generate growth and greater uncertainty for economic actors facing rapidly changing markets and production processes. Work reorganisation, in its many dimensions from teams and non-hierarchical workplaces to decentralisation and telecommuting entrepreneurs, is expected to be one of the fundamental growth forces likely to demand new ways of managing individual, corporate and social risks. Technological developments, and not only in the fields of computers and telecommunications, will encourage growth while also contributing to turbulent and unanticipated changes in what, how and where people produce and consume. Continued globalisation, with its greater interdependence and positive impact on technology diffusion, trade and growth in general, will also demand considerable economic, social and even cultural adaptation. Lastly, as governments reduce the constraints on market forces and focus increasingly on framework policies instead of direct intervention, the actual growth trajectory will come to depend to an even greater extent on how the private sector responds.

Yet, as a few participants pointed out, the rate and scale of adaptation necessary to meet the exacting requirements of a dynamic and highly flexible economy will still depend, at least partially, on the pace of economic growth. Weaker growth could bring with it the risk of social strife and a disintegration of the economic policy consensus. Stronger growth rates might ease somewhat the pressures to adapt and at the same time provide greater room to manoeuvre. However, given the widely held expectation of only modest long-run growth, there is likely to be a fairly urgent need to develop mechanisms of economic and social risk management that correspond to conditions of greater flexibility and turbulence. Indeed, the adoption of broad, new approaches to ensuring complementarity instead of dissonance between economic and social conditions is already considered to be high on the agenda of firms, governments and many individuals.

A renewed role for governance

Adapting to the intensive and unsettling transformations that are likely both to accompany and spur economic growth in the future will probably put greater emphasis on the renewal of decision-making and participatory processes. As a number of conference participants stressed, it will be important to improve systems of governance, not only in the democratic fora of the political sphere, but also in enterprises and communities where many of the crucial decisions will be made on a daily basis. The private sector is already pointing the way with organisational restructuring that moves away from hierarchical methods of command and control.

Drawing together the threads of the discussion, it is anticipated that enhancing the democratic infrastructure of OECD societies will offer a threefold dividend. First, better governance methods are likely both to enable and sustain a respect for people's differences in the context of a convergence towards a common economic environment characterised by freer markets. Secondly, there is likely to be an indispensable synergy between governance systems that encourage social responsibility and the trust needed for the success of both a decentralised, innovation-driven economy and more flexible social orders. Finally, the evolution of governance systems towards greater sharing of responsibility at work and in the community might encourage public perceptions of the potential for a win/win outcome from the turbulence of the flexible economy. Governance reform could be one way of trying to make sure that the active promotion of social inclusion or participation is part of any new and innovative approaches to finding the balance between societal cohesion and economic flexibility.

Reorienting the welfare state

Participants were largely of the view that considerable renovation would be needed in the programmes and institutions of the welfare state as a consequence of changes in the underlying needs of client populations, altered fiscal circumstances and production process breakthroughs that promise greater efficiency in the delivery of social services. Whether such reforms can successfully follow an incremental path or, in view of the degree of change required, will need to make a more radical break with past practices remains an open question. Here, as already noted, economic growth rates were viewed as likely to influence the required pace, if not the ultimate scope, of adaptation.

Extensive discussion and disagreement surrounded the role of existing institutions, particularly the welfare state, in aggravating rather than attenuating the friction between societal cohesion and economic flexibility in the future. These differing views were also reflected in assessments of the extent to which incremental social policy reforms, already largely under way, will be adequate to the task of fostering adaptability in an ever-more turbulent environment. Those with a more sanguine perspective considered the gradual reform and basic continuity of existing welfare, social security, health and education systems as sufficient. They considered that incremental administrative and programme reform in the public sector would allow it to continue in its role as primary direct provider of social services without the danger of excessive inflexibility or uniformity.

For other conference participants, societal cohesion is likely to be menaced by the perverse tendency of certain social programmes to incite dependency while fiscal retrenchment undermines the available resources. This phenomenon, called the "quicksand effect", could undermine efforts to develop more efficient social insurance schemes that align individual costs and benefits. From this perspective, more transparent mechanisms for insuring people against economic and social risks, involving potentially significant breaks with the traditional mechanisms of the welfare state, will be indispensable for achieving the combination of adaptability and sense of security required by the dynamic and highly diverse economy of the future.

Towards universal rights and individualised programmes

In general, the discussion pointed towards a less dominant role for government in securing societal cohesion in the context of a comprehensive strategy based on the extension of universal rights and the pursuit of policies that offer individuals greater choice and self-determination. Different variants of such a strategy might place more or less emphasis on collective public institutions, depending on the political choices and values of society. Still, all of the approaches discussed share the common characteristic of aiming to foster a more adaptable economy, able to bend and change according to the imperatives of innovation and competition.

In practical terms, much of the work to secure societal cohesion is expected to continue to occur – in many cases to an even greater degree – outside the institutions and programmes provided directly by government. Households, workplaces and voluntary associations will maintain a central role in providing citizens with a sense of security, belonging and identity. But with much greater diversity anticipated in the types of households, workplaces and voluntary associations of the future, governments will likely be called upon to move towards creating frameworks and basic standards, and away from the direct provision of uniform services.

The policy challenge is therefore expected to lie squarely in the realm of fostering such autonomy without either blunting the signals and incentives of the market or losing the social solidarity required for effective collaboration and a sharing of basic aspirations. Workable balances will, in the view of most conference participants, differ considerably across OECD nations and regions in accordance with distinct values and traditions. Allowing for such differences while seeking congruence and avoiding conflicts with international obligations will call for mutual understanding and co-operation.

Innovative approaches to finding the balance between economic flexibility and societal cohesion

A wide range of innovative responses to the challenge of societal cohesion in the 21st century were aired at the conference. The proposals can be grouped into four distinct areas. First, conference participants agreed that important changes will need to be made to the systems used for insuring citizens against risks such as unemployment, disease, disability and poverty. Proposals discussed at the conference envisaged the possibility of citizens opting out of public schemes and services or gaining access to government loan guarantees for personal investment purposes, e.g. education. Such reforms would provide clearer incentives to save, work and invest while helping to avoid the problems of moral hazard and poverty traps. Properly designed, a more diversified and transparent approach to economic and social insurance could also spur the development of more effective risk reduction strategies, even for the chronically poor. These new insurance schemes of a public, private or mixed character might be more efficient, not only because there would be a better correspondence with the great diversity of risk profiles, but also due to a better responsiveness to the uncertainties generated by a flexible economy.

A second set of crucial changes concerns learning systems in general and the more narrow question of urgently reforming existing state-dominated education. Again, the most fruitful direction points towards greater recognition of diversity and improvements in transparency. Practically, this should lead to better validation of different types of learning throughout life (home, school, work) and clearer incentives for investing (even on borrowed financing) in the accumulation of human capital. In much the same way as firms are reorganising work and business strategy, sources and uses of learning could be more diversified, decentralised and "consumer"-driven.

A third group of institutional and social adaptations that could contribute to securing societal cohesion in the future centre on what might be called responsibility systems. Here, innovation is called for in the areas of corporate and local community governance. Conference participants judged methods for spurring commitment, involvement and long-term thinking to be critical components of tomorrow's more decentralised yet interdependent world. For managers, workers and the surrounding localities, not to mention investors, the evolution of corporate and local governance systems would attempt to compensate for the decline in traditional methods of encouraging responsibility, e.g. lifetime employment contracts and detailed direct regulatory constraints.

Lastly, and controversially, there were those who argued for a major transformation of the economic and social importance attached to paid employment. This fourth approach would involve the introduction of a universal citizen's income intended to put greater value on the broad range of human activities that extends well beyond paid work. On the one hand, worries were expressed about both affordability and the perverse incentive effects that might arise if paid employment and income were delinked. On the other hand, it was acknowledged that for many people employment of any kind, let alone work at above poverty-level wages, might not be attainable – particularly if economic growth does turn out to be quite modest. More general support was offered for policies that validate a broad range of human activities without inhibiting the decline in the share of traditional full-time, lifetime jobs. Finally, since work of all kinds, paid and unpaid, will continue to be central to achieving social integration, policies should be crafted so as to encourage activities such as environmental conservation, community care and learning.

Future OECD contributions

Overall, the many possible ways of achieving a functional balance between economic flexibility and societal cohesion can be seen as ways of building up a more robust, adaptable society able to cope with future shifts – in employment patterns, in the degree and nature of uncertainty, and in traditional approaches to social inclusion. Viewing this broad and multi-disciplinary landscape, conference participants urged a continuing active role for the OECD in three areas: first, in developing a deeper understanding of the interaction between economic perform-ance and societal cohesion; second, in conducting rigorous analyses of available policy options and providing comparative benchmarks of best-practices; and third, in encouraging open discussion of potential friction between one nation's efforts at combining economic flexibility with societal cohesion and those undertaken either by other countries individually or by the international community more generally.

Finally, the conference debate underscored the importance of taking into account all of the elements that underpin societal cohesion, especially since such a broad perspective promises to reintroduce a critical if at times ignored factor: the political process. Much discussion naturally focuses on the rapid rates of techno-logical change, continuing liberalisation of trade and investment, and the push towards an increasingly knowledge-based economy marked by the growing influ-ence of market forces and global competition. However, as the discussion showed, successfully knitting together a viable social fabric from this turbulent process will hinge on the capacity of political institutions to develop solutions appropriate to a world where uncertainty and unpredictability seem destined to grow. Governments will not be alone in the effort to forge societal cohesion since firms, households and the many cultural and social organisations of everyday life will also contribute. It should be possible to find distinctive ways, respectful of different values and aspira-tions, for striking a durable balance between economic flexibility and societal cohesion.

2

CURRENT ECONOMIC POLICIES: SOCIAL IMPLICATIONS OVER THE LONGER TERM

by
Robert Z. Lawrence
John F. Kennedy School of Government
Harvard University

This paper surveys economic performance and policies in the OECD over the postwar period and offers three possible future scenarios. It considers the social implications of implementing the current policy trinity – monetary restraint, fiscal retrenchment and market liberalisation. In a slow-growth environment, citizens feel an increased need for government assistance, but the government is less able to provide it. Outcomes therefore depend increasingly on private sector responses. The central message of the paper is that while the effects of policies may be important, the exogenous forces which drive the economy, such as technology and demographics, and private sector responses to those forces will play a crucial role in determining if the outcome is best described as "doldrums", "cyber-euphoria", or "black judgement".

THE PAST

The golden era in the first twenty-five years of the postwar period gave rise to heightened expectations about economic performance. Between 1950 and 1973, per capita incomes in the United States grew more rapidly than in any previous quarter-century – averaging 2.2 per cent annually. Yet Europe and Japan grew even faster. Europe closed much of the gap in per capita incomes between it and the United States. Japan, starting from much lower income levels, did likewise, completing the transition from developing to developed economy.

Welfare state. As growth exceeded expectations, the welfare state expanded. Governments sought to provide not only basic benefits for the poor, but broad support for housing, health, education and retirement. In a Europe driven by the desire for a solidaristic "social wage", most measures were not means tested, whereas in the United States means testing was more common. Nonetheless, throughout the OECD area, social expenditures on education, health, social security and welfare grew rapidly, typically increasing the share of such spending in GDP between 1960 and 1975 by about 10 percentage points. Associated with the rise in government social transfers was an increase in taxes, particularly those imposed on employment.

Market intervention. Governments also assumed increasing obligations for economic outcomes beyond achieving full employment. In Europe, governments frequently tried to maintain employment in particular regions, firms and even jobs. Traditional regulatory objectives, such as safety on the job, and other rules governing employment were expanded. In both Europe and Japan, the state also implemented industrial policies to promote industries of the future and to aid those in decline. When market forces seemed inadequate, states nationalised private firms, allocated credit, encouraged mergers, nurtured national champion firms and, in Europe, operated state-owned industries. In the United States, policies were more *laissez-faire*, but the government did intervene occasionally to bale out troubled firms and protect troubled industries.

Corporate obligations. In an environment of prosperity in which growth was driven by economies of scale, private firms also increased their explicit and implicit obligations to their workers and other stakeholders. In Japan, in particular, the invisible hand was strongly mediated by the invisible handshake: large firms provided lifetime employment and were linked to other firms through groups known as *keiretsu* which were often centered around key large banks. In European countries these relationships were more likely to be enshrined explicitly in laws and regulations, and legislative action was taken in several countries to ensure worker participation in management decision-making and government oversight of plant closures and lay-offs. Even in the United States, it was not unknown for large firms such as IBM and Delta Airlines to offer implicit guarantees of lifetime employment. While elements were shared throughout the OECD, it seems reasonable to state that the welfare state was most extensively developed in Europe, and the network of implicit obligations most extensively developed in Japan.

Stagflation. In the early 1970s, however, growth slowed and wage demands outpaced output growth. In 1973, in a highly inflationary outburst, synchronised global expansion and soaring commodity prices heralded a new era of stagflation. Growth has declined throughout the developed world – the pace between 1973 and 1990 was typically about a third slower than in the 1950s and 1960s. This slow growth reflected a universal decline in productivity growth. Growth has also been more volatile; bouts of inflation have been followed by severe cyclical downturns. Inflation has been kept in check in the 1990s, but growth has been even slower than between 1973 and 1990.

Slow growth. The growth slowdowns have taken different forms. In the United States, employment has increased steadily but average wages have grown very slowly.[1] In Europe, by contrast, output per worker and real wages have risen steadily, although more slowly than in the 50s and 60s – but unemployment has increased and labour force participation has fallen.[2] Japan fared considerably better in sustaining both real-wage growth and employment growth until the early 1990s. More recently, however, it has experienced stagnation and growing overt and disguised unemployment.

Inequality. In the United States, incomes have not only grown slowly; they have become less equal. This is evident in measures of household incomes, wages and wealth. While households in the upper quintile have enjoyed income growth, the lowest three quintiles have experienced absolute declines. Wage data display similar patterns whether grouped by education, occupation or skills. Moreover, a substantial increase in inequality has also occurred among workers with similar educational, occupational and industry backgrounds. The combination of slow average wage growth and rising inequality has actually meant a real decline in the wages of less-skilled American workers – indeed, real average hourly earnings in 1996 are no higher than they were in the mid-1960s.

Poverty. These developments have taken their toll on poverty rates. As noted in the 1995 *Economic Report of the President* (p. 178), between 1960 and 1973 poverty in the United States fell from 22 to 11 per cent; it then increased to 15 per cent by 1993 – *i.e.* reversing 36 per cent of the gains. Poverty rates for children fell from 27 per cent in 1960 to 14 per cent in 1973, and then rose to 23 per cent in 1993 – reversing 70 per cent of the gains. To be sure, the plight of poor children is affected not only by earnings but also by the rise of single-parent families and by the 20 per cent decline in inflation-adjusted benefits between 1972 and the mid-1980s. There has also been a noteworthy reversal of the progress made between 1962 and 1973 in closing some of the gap in earnings between white and black Americans, and a noteworthy decline in black male labour force participation.

Rising inequality is evident in other English-speaking developed economies – the United Kingdom, Canada, Australia and New Zealand. In continental Europe, however, wage differentials were either broadly unchanged or increased only slightly. There is evidence of only small increases in the premiums on schooling and in the age-earnings profiles in some European countries.

Unemployment. Since 1973, European countries have experienced high levels of unemployment particularly concentrated on younger workers and those out of jobs for more than twelve months. An important question is the degree to which institutional and regulatory factors in Europe have repressed wage adjustments, impaired work incentives, raised unemployment and slowed labour force growth. The comprehensive *OECD Jobs Study*, for example, concludes that all developed countries have experienced a shift in demand away from unskilled jobs. In countries where relative wages have been flexible, both relative employment and unemployment rates of the unskilled changed little during the 1980s. In countries with less wage flexibility, the effects have been felt in employment performance. In Japan, until the 1990s, neither unemployment nor a rise in inequality was particularly evident. In the 1990s, however, unemployment and disguised unemployment have increased.

Restructuring. Throughout the developed world, corporations have experienced wrenching changes. Employment in large corporations has declined dramatically. In the United States for example, while the labour force has grown rapidly, employment in the Fortune 500 companies declined from 17 million in 1980 to 11.5 million currently. Companies have slimmed down to their core competencies, outsourcing many activities to smaller firms and to other countries. The result has been a decline in the importance of internal allocation mechanisms and an increased use of market mechanisms. In addition, heightened competition has forced firms to reduce their commitments to providing workers with employment stability and security. Deregulation has limited the capacity of firms to cross-subsidise activities that are not viable with rents earned in activities in which they have market power.

Explanations. The sources of these problems are not well understood. Despite its economic importance, the productivity slowdown has not been given the research attention it deserves. With the wisdom of hindsight, at least, some of this slower growth might have been expected. In the 1950s and 1960s, the United States had enjoyed access to an unusually large residue of innovations which depression and war had prevented from being fully exploited. In Europe and Japan, the exhaustion of the benefits of relative backwardness that came from adopting readily available US know-how played an additional role in the slowdown. But productivity growth has been even slower than an extrapolation of earlier historical trends would have predicted.[3]

The sources of growing inequality in the United States and unemployment among the unskilled in Europe are also hotly debated. In both Europe and the United States, alarms have been sounded about the role of trade and international investment in shifting the demand for unskilled labour. In the United States, the debate over the NAFTA in the early 1990s crystallised concerns over wage performance that are best captured by Ross Perot's allusion to the "giant sucking sound" of jobs as they move southward.

In Europe, the recessionary environment of the 90s sparked similar fears of "delocalisation", *i.e.* that firms are relocating to low-wage countries. In Japan, the debate has become particularly heated in recent years, where it is couched as a concern about the hollowing out of the economy. The Japanese have not seen an increase in inequality, but there are fears that Japanese industry is caught in a squeeze: as newly industrialising economies move into basic manufacturing industries which Japan once dominated, Japan itself has been unsuccessful in entering high-technology industries of the future such as software finance and advanced micro-processors. The strengthening of the yen in the mid-1980s initiated these concerns as Japanese manufacturers began to invest outside the country in increasing numbers. After a period of respite in which a booming domestic economy laid some of these fears to rest, the association of slow growth and a strong yen have again brought them to the fore. As Japanese firms increasingly relocate abroad, fear is voiced about the ability of Japanese manufacturers to maintain their basic institutions such as lifetime employment and strong corporate groups. Most economists argue, however, that these pressures on unskilled labour are more powerfully driven by skill-biased technological change. In particular, technology appears to have shifted towards requiring the more intensive use of skilled and educated workers. The spread of computers, information technology and new forms of labour-management relations may also have been important.

Policy impotence. It is not easy for governments to address the problems of slow growth, structural unemployment and increasing inequality. To stimulate growth, increased investment is required; however, the payoffs from increases on a feasible scale are unlikely to be large compared with the size of the slowdown, and could take a considerable amount of time to become perceptible. In the short run, taking these steps requires additional reductions in public and private consumption, neither of which are attractive in a slow-growth economy.

Undertaking structural reforms is equally difficult. In Europe, for example, tackling structural unemployment is often seen as requiring increased labour market flexibility. Recommended measures such as reducing subsidies, payroll taxes and minimum wages and relaxing labour market regulations and other rules all face considerable political resistance, particularly during periods of high unemployment. In Japan, similarly, reforms require deregulation, market-opening and a reduction in the power of government bureaucracy – again, measures supported by powerful vested interests. Trying to reverse the trends in trade and/or technology could well further damage improvements in overall living standards. Nor is it simple to reduce inequality directly through income redistribution. In the United States, the most significant redistribution of the income pie has actually been among workers rather than between capital and labour. Again, solving this problem honestly is particularly difficult, since it requires redistribution not from a relatively small class of capitalists but from the much more powerful intellectual elite.

The policy trinity. It has therefore been difficult, in these environments, for governments and firms to honour the commitments they assumed during more prosperous periods. Policies have cycled, between measures to avoid change and measures to adjust to it. Initially governments tried to boost growth through expansionary monetary policies, but the result was simply higher inflation. Inevitably, monetary restraint followed. Initially governments tried to stabilize employment, maintain entitlements and aid firms and workers in distress. Inevitably, lay-offs, cuts in aid and fiscal retrenchment followed. Similarly, regulatory efforts to prevent change and protect domestic industries have been followed by deregulation, privatisation, and trade and international financial liberalisation. The result is the current economic environment, in which policies are characterised by three elements: *a)* commitment to monetary stability; *b)* widespread fiscal retrenchment; and *c)* measures reducing the role of the government in regulating or participating in the economy, and a correspondingly increased role for markets in resource allocation.

THE FUTURE

It is likely that, at least for the foreseeable future, the constraints on government that have induced the policy trinity are likely to prevail. Indeed, they may well become tighter. One driver in the future will be demography. Although the pressures will be felt to differing degrees, throughout the OECD area it is anticipated that labour force growth will decline and the retired cohorts will grow. The latter raises the demands for government welfare spending, while the former reduces the capacity for supplying it. If growth continues at rates that are currently projected, therefore, fiscal retrenchment in particular is likely to be a permanent feature of the environment. In addition, in Europe, the need to meet the Maastricht criteria will be an additional impulse for both fiscal and monetary restraint. It is highly unlikely, therefore, that social welfare programmes will be expanded or that governments will play any larger roles in redistributing income from rich to poor or in providing increased social expenditures. In addition, the trend toward deregulation and liberalisation is likely to continue. In Europe, efforts to inject flexibility into labour markets will continue, as will deregulation in Japan. Similarly, even without new agreements, commitments to trade liberalisation made at the Uruguay Round and in regional arrangements are likely to be fulfilled.

If these current economic trends do continue, governments will be less able to directly determine the economic fortunes of their citizens. Economies will be more open, and government fiscal policies tightly constrained. At the same time, heightened competition will force firms to re-examine their commitments to their workforce.

The fate of citizens, particularly the poor, will therefore rest heavily not on government performance but rather on the performance of market forces. And this is not easy to predict. The uncertainties are associated with the likely impact of exogenous forces and of responses to current policies that will drive the economy.

The first uncertainty relates to the pressures on the earnings of unskilled workers. With regard to demand, the impacts of technological change and international trade are likely to be important. On the one hand, skill premiums could decline further (and/or structural unemployment worsen) if technical change continues to be biased against unskilled workers. Similarly, unskilled workers could be adversely affected by competition from developing countries whose presence in global markets will be increasingly felt. On the other hand, demand could shift in favour of less-skilled workers if firms are induced by the declining relative cost of unskilled workers to develop technologies that employ unskilled workers more intensively. Downward wage pressures could also be relieved if unskilled workers increasingly shift into jobs with firms that do not produce goods and services which compete directly with those from developing countries. In addition, an increase in the relative supply of skilled workers could reduce skill premiums if workers are induced by the rise in the skill premium to raise their investments in education and other forms of human capital.

A second uncertainty relates to the impact of technological and other innovations on productivity growth. A plausible argument can be made that the full benefits of new information technologies will take time to be realised. In particular, the task is not simply to diffuse new technologies but also to undertake the institutional and social changes that will allow their full exploitation. The current phase is one of major restructuring but hopefully, once the effort has been made, the payoff will be in higher growth. In the United States in particular, the restoration of productivity growth in the services sector would be particularly important. Faster growth could dramatically alter the fiscal environment, permitting the maintenance and possibly the expansion of social welfare and other programmes.

Another key factor is the payoff in the form of increased growth as a result of current policy measures. In Europe, measures to improve labour market flexibility could reduce structural unemployment. In Japan, deregulation could lead to faster productivity growth in sectors where innovation is currently repressed. And throughout the OECD area, continued liberalisation in trade and investment could lead to more rapid growth. However, current policies could also damage growth. First, stringent fiscal and monetary policies could retard economies in achieving full employment. In addition, there is a danger that the reduction in fiscal deficits could be achieved through measures which increase marginal tax rates on both labour and capital, which could in turn reduce growth. There is also a danger that changes in regulatory approaches could lead to less rather than more efficient outcomes, either because such efforts are effectively captured by vested interests or simply because of policy errors. These considerations suggest that to explore the social welfare implications of a continuation of current policies, three scenarios might be useful.

Scenarios

In the first and most likely scenario, *the doldrums*, growth occurs at the mediocre rates currently anticipated. The second scenario, plausible but considerably less likely, is *cyber-euphoria*, in which technological innovation and successful policies raise long-run productivity growth rates back to postwar average rates. The third, again possible but even less likely, is *black judgement*, in which growth is even slower and more volatile. The social welfare implications of each are examined below.

The doldrums

The most likely scenario for the next fifteen years is based on current projections. The most plausible of these is that slow growth will continue, at least through the end of the decade. According to the Bureau of Labor Statistics, between 1995 and 2005 the US labour force will grow at just over 1 per cent annually – half the pace recorded in the late 1970s. (The labour force is expected to grow even more slowly thereafter, actually declining at 0.2 per cent annually between 2010 and 2030.) Adding these labour force projections to the 1 per cent annual growth in productivity suggests that potential US GDP is growing at just over 2 per cent.[4] In the medium term both Europe and Japan may have more room than the United States to grow by reducing unemployment. According to estimates of the OECD, between 1997 and 2000 for example, growth rates of 3 and 3.8 per cent annually could be achieved in Europe and Japan respectively.[5] But once cyclical unemployment is eliminated, the OECD estimates potential growth at 2.75 and 3 per cent in Europe and Japan respectively, and structural unemployment in Europe remains high at around 9.5 per cent.[6]

In this scenario, therefore, incomes throughout OECD countries rise slowly, reflecting limited gains from technology and globalisation. In the United States, growth slows gradually to around 1.5 per cent near the end of the period. Overall, average real wages and per capita incomes increase, but by less than 1 per cent annually. Poverty rates rise and the unskilled see their compensation levels remaining flat. US inequality thus rises in an environment of slow growth. This inevitably exacerbates the plight of black Americans. At the same time, employment increases – although undoubtedly there are cycles and periods in which unemployment rises to between 7 and 8 per cent. Under this scenario, those particularly reliant on government programmes experience a deterioration in their circumstances. Welfare programmes in the United States have recently been reduced and work requirements have been increased. Within five years, a large number of recipients could therefore be ineligible, thereby contributing to increased hardship and poverty. In addition, the Medicare programme in the United States is not sustainable currently and the social security fund would similarly run into solvency problems in a few decades unless something is done. There is a strong resistance to tax increases. It is therefore likely that benefits will be reduced.

In Europe, under this scenario structural unemployment remains high and, as in the United States, there are strong pressures to reduce social safety nets. But real wages grow at rates of between 1 and 2 per cent annually and, reflecting the strong support which it commands, the social safety net – although reduced – is still maintained at high levels. High structural unemployment falls particularly on the young, the old and less-skilled workers. Social problems increase, but again remain within politically tolerable limits.

In an environment of slow growth and high unemployment, European-level government is not particularly popular. Indeed, the constraints placed on national fiscal policies by the Maastricht criteria make the Commission in particular and the EU in general a convenient scapegoat. In addition, Europe will find it highly challenging to broaden the community's membership in a slow-growth environment. As in the United States, racial tensions associated with new immigrants and minorities increase.

In Japan, real-income growth, although much slower than that achieved in the 1980s, is more rapid than in the rest of the OECD area. This gives rise to sustained improvements in living standards. In addition, continued progress in deregulation and liberalisation improves consumer choice. However, government benefits are reduced and corporations reduce the extent of their long-term relationships with stakeholders. In particular, *keiretsu* relationships, particularly those not justified by efficiency considerations, become somewhat weaker. Lay-offs become more common and opportunities for young educated workers in large, premier Japanese corporations decline. Deregulation also puts downward pressure on small shop-keepers and wages in highly sheltered sectors. Overall, however, the invisible hand-shake continues to exert far more influence in Japan than in other OECD economies.

In sum, while this may not be an explosive scenario, there are several elements in it that are disquieting. The bulk of Americans could experience some improvements in living standards – although at rates much slower than over the previous century – but the plight of the poorest Americans worsens. Similarly, while the material conditions of most Europeans improve, significant elements of European society are excluded from participation in the labour market, supported in only modest fashion by state funds. And in Japan, most citizens find their living standards rising, but there are significant pressures on existing institutions.

Cyber-euphoria

The combination of prudent policies, technological innovation and globalisation pay off beyond current expectations. Throughout OECD countries growth begins to accelerate in the early twenty-first century. Governments discover revenues exceeding expectations. The entire OECD area enjoys benefits from trade with and investment in the emerging economies. Import prices fall and because Member countries have completed their adjustment out of standardized production activities, this trade benefits even the least-skilled workers. In the environment of prosperity, a new initiative, OECD 2020, is launched to construct a single market for goods, services and capital throughout the developed world. The WTO members pledge they will achieve free trade in the same year.

In the United States, education reform pays off. Productivity improvements of fairly large orders of magnitude are finally experienced in the services sector. The Internet allows for many virtual companies in which workers are linked together in activities that yield large increases in productivity. Per capita incomes rise at 2 per cent annually and because larger numbers of Americans obtain college degrees, the skill premium shrinks so that the poor and unskilled enjoy even greater increases. Poverty rates fall back to levels achieved in the early 1970s. Firms have already slimmed down to their competitive cores. With aggregate demand growing more rapidly, relatively fewer firms are compelled to downsize. Firms increase their implicit long-term commitments to workers.

In Europe, as labour markets are freed up, structural unemployment rates decline. Employment opportunities, particularly for young Europeans, grow rapidly. Government fiscal positions are unexpectedly healthy, not simply because of higher revenues deriving from faster productivity growth, but also because of increased tax payments by previously unemployed workers. At the same time, spending on welfare and unemployment declines even though benefit levels are improved. The European central bank feels free to relax monetary policy and discovers to the delight of all that the NAIRU has fallen throughout Europe. Given the relaxation of fiscal constraints, southern European economies join in the Monetary Union. In the euphoria of the new millennium, Europe embraces a host of new members and uses the revenue surplus to buy out farmers in a one-time deal to permanently downsize the Common Agricultural Policy.

In Japan, a new generation of dynamic entrepreneurs in medium-size firms are nurtured by a growing venture capital sector, while large firms find it possible to maintain lifetime employment because of strong demand growth due to expanding domestic and foreign, particularly Asian, markets. Deregulation gives rise to major improvements in product choice and price. The combination of strong demand and slow labour force growth creates shortages of workers which are met by increasing imports of labour-intensive products. Major initiatives shift farmers off the land and thus free up farmland for housing and recreational purposes, while reformed and more market-oriented traditional institutions survive.

Black judgement

Productivity growth slows even further than in the first scenario and the new technologies create disruption and dislocation. By the start of the new millennium the need for fiscal retrenchments is even greater than it is today. The European central bank, intent on establishing its credibility, follows an extremely Draconian monetary policy. Global recession results. Radical populist groups emerge through-out OECD countries, pressing protectionist agendas. In response to high unemploy-ment in Europe, growing unemployment in Japan, and falling wages of less-skilled Americans, a moratorium is placed on additional imports from the developing countries. Multinational firms, reliant on global sourcing, are forced to contract. Stock markets plummet as trade barriers are raised in developing countries in efforts to preserve foreign exchange reserves and avoid debt and financial crises.

In the United States the slowdown in productivity growth reduces potential growth to around one and a half per cent, and per capita growth to around half a per cent per year. Large numbers of Americans experience declining real wages. Welfare programmes are severely cut back, and social security and Medicare entitlements are dramatically reduced. Poverty rates soar. Immigration is halted. Large numbers of homeless women and their children flock into shelters created out of unused factories. Social tensions rise. Race riots are fairly common.

In Europe the efforts to rein in the welfare state set off a downward spiral. Benefits are maintained by raising payroll taxes in the face of slow growth and high unemployment. This in turn further raises structural unemployment. While the extremes of poverty in the United States are avoided, even middle-class Europeans experience long periods in which their real incomes are stagnant. Large numbers of alienated youths pursue alternative lifestyles. There are also racial tensions against new immigrants. Several countries vote to leave the European Monetary Union.

In Japan, firms are forced by their poor earnings growth eventually to lay off large numbers of prime male workers. The unemployment rate moves into ranges typical of the United States. The movement towards deregulation is stopped and large numbers of cartels are formed in efforts to prevent even further erosion of profits and financial crises.

CONCLUDING COMMENT

What appears striking from this analysis is the variety of plausible outcomes which could emerge given current policies. This reflects the fact that the policy stance currently prevailing inceases the role for market forces and reduces the role of government intervention. While the most likely scenario is an environment in which current trends prevail, there are certainly possibilities that are far better – and far worse.

NOTES

1. In the United States the impact of slower productivity on consumption growth between 1973 and 1990 was limited by faster labour force growth and increased borrowing. But by the early 1990s the baby boom generation had long been absorbed into the workforce, and female participation rates levelled out. In the 90s US spending patterns have been aligned more closely to incomes. In particular, the federal budget deficit has been reduced. The result has been a very slow rise in per capita incomes.

2. Because of slow employment growth, between 1980 and 1995 output per working-age person in Europe has actually grown more slowly than in the United States. (See *OECD Economic Outlook*, June 1996, page 22.)

3. The slowdown in the United States is particularly evident in sectors outside of manufacturing. But this is perplexing given the rapid increase in the use of computers, which might have been expected to be particularly beneficial in the services sector. It seems that the full potential of the computer is not being realised. Equally perplexing is the fact that major corporate restructuring and downsizing do not seem to have raised productivity.

4. In the absence of faster productivity growth, an economy can exceed its potential growth pace only by reducing unemployment. By 1996, however, according to most observers – and, more importantly, the Federal Reserve Board – US growth is constrained by a sluggishly expanding potential. Even if the economy actually has scope to reduce unemployment by another percentage point before inflation accelerates, this one-time gain leaves the long-run problem unaffected.

5. *OECD Economic Outlook*, December 1994, page 27.

6. Ibid, page 27.

3

CHALLENGES TO SOCIAL COHESION
AND APPROACHES TO POLICY REFORM

by

Dennis J. Snower
Department of Economics, Birkbeck College
University of London

Now, at the end of the twentieth century, many OECD countries face serious problems in achieving both prosperity and social cohesion. One important – and sadly neglected – source of these problems lies within the very policy systems meant to address them. Those systems – including taxes and transfers, regulations governing employment, welfare services, and many more – are imparting a serious long-term imbalance to their host countries by making them increasingly vulnerable to economic, social and political shocks. Although such systems were originally designed with the express aim of cushioning citizens from such shocks and providing security against a variety of uncertainties, their long-term effect is turning out to be the opposite of what was intended.

This paper examines how and why this has happened and then turns to some important recent economic developments that are likely to make the problem worse in the future. Finally, it examines a strategy for economic policy reform that addresses the problem and thereby provides a means for achieving more favourable economic and social outcomes in the years ahead.

POLICY SYSTEMS AS A SOURCE OF IMBALANCE IN THE OECD

The central pillars of the main OECD policy systems – unemployment benefit systems, job security regulations, networks of taxes and transfers, pension systems, health and education systems, and various other groups of welfare state entitlements – were erected in the golden years of the 1950s and 60s, when economic growth was high, the labour force was increasing, unemployment was low, and poverty was falling. Thanks to this propitious economic performance, only a small minority of citizens required the support that the welfare states were offering, and even when they did so, the need was often only temporary. Under these circumstances, it was possible for governments to be generous in providing support for the poor, benefits for the unemployed, pensions for the elderly, education for the young, and health care for the sick.

With the upsurge in economic activity, a large group of tax-paying, employed people helped support a relatively small group of unemployed ones; a large group of healthy people provided for a small group of unhealthy and disabled ones. As populations and labour forces grew, a relatively large group of young people financed the pensions of a relatively small group of retirees. In short, the prevailing economic policy systems were able to provide substantial economic security and protection against poverty as long as little reliance was placed on these systems.

But the services of these systems have been important to most people's well-being even when they were not used. An important reason is that people often get stuck in unfavourable economic and social states unless they receive prompt help in overcoming them. Those who become ill may remain unhealthy unless they receive prompt treatment; people who fall into poverty may remain there unless they receive some support to improve their skills and gain appropriate employment; people who become unemployed require prompt incentives to find work again, before they become deskilled, unmotivated, and stigmatised. In these various ways, welfare state policy systems made important contributions to prosperity and social cohesion, even though only a relatively small minority of the population made use of them at any given point in time.

In a sense, these policy systems played a role similar to fire insurance in making a significant contribution to one's peace of mind even when one's house has not burned down. Their ability to cushion people from economic uncertainties and to correct glaring market failures in the provision of education, health insurance, unemployment insurance and pensions doubtlessly played an important role in promoting the postwar prosperity. Public support for education helped raise people 's skills; job security legislation helped bond employers to their employees and thereby gave both parties incentives to invest in training; unemployment benefits gave the temporarily jobless people the means to search for the appropriate jobs, rather than accepting the first position that came along; public health provision helped promote a healthier, and hence more productive, workforce; income redistribution systems and poverty programmes helped create more cohesive societies and reduce social polarisation along with the associated costs of crime and social tension.

In these many ways, the welfare states amplified the favourable economic and social conditions most OECD countries faced in the early postwar years.

But then, around the mid-1970s, the party came to an end. After the first oil price shock in 1973, trend productivity growth in most market economies fell sharply and, despite subsequent booms and periods of optimism, has not recovered since then. As a result, poverty became a more challenging problem and income redistribution, to meet this problem, became more painful. As the postwar baby boom subsided, population growth slowed, particularly in Europe. This meant that the people of working age were required to support an increasingly larger proportion of older people. In addition, the increasingly generous pensions, which the retirees were unable to bequeath to their children, reduced people's incentive to save, and stimulated consumption at the expense of capital accumulation. Furthermore, the long recessions of the mid-1970s, early 1980s and early 1990s – interacting with the European nexus of stringent job security provisions and generous unemployment benefits – made European unemployment rates drift inexorably upwards, from an average EC rate of 3.7 per cent in the 1970s, to 9.1 per cent in the 1980s, to around 11 per cent now. Thus unemployment benefits and income support, which were originally designed to tide people over temporary jobless spells, became their mainstay over many years and, in some cases, the basis for an unemployed way of life. In Europe, therefore, the employed taxpayers were required to support a growing segment of unemployed claimants.

On account of these developments, welfare state spending rose rapidly as a percentage of GNP in Europe and most other OECD areas. This rise in spending, combined with the shrinking tax base, made it necessary for governments to raise taxes and public borrowing. Increasingly, these governments found it difficult to meet their commitments in supporting education, health, disability, housing, unemployment insurance and pensions. The increasing taxes on employers discouraged job creation, the increasing taxes on employees discouraged job search, the increasing taxes on non-wage incomes and wealth discouraged saving and capital accumulation. Public borrowing put upward pressure on real interest rates, thereby discouraging capital accumulation even more.

After about a decade of these developments, it was virtually inevitable that governments in many OECD countries should find themselves confronted by an overwhelming need for retrenchment in the 1980s. The pace and scale of this retrenchment process varied considerably among the OECD countries and were dictated profoundly by voting arithmetic. As a result, the process turned out to be highly asymmetric. Since the poor and the unemployed are generally not a large or influential segment of the voting population, it has often been easier for governments to relinquish previous commitments to these groups than to the middle classes. Thus, in many OECD countries, eligibility criteria for unemployment benefits and income support were tightened, monitoring procedures for the fulfilment of these criteria became more stringent, regulations were relaxed to allow greater scope for temporary, part-time, and self-employment, and the growth of various poverty programmes was arrested or rolled back. On the other hand, public spending on pensions and (to a somewhat lesser degree) on education and health has been largely unaffected by the drive towards fiscal austerity. Job security legislation protecting the positions of the established, incumbent employees was also left largely intact.

As a result, governments became progressively less able to protect their citizens from economic uncertainties – just at the time when these uncertainties were growing. A wide variety of forces – including the liberalisation of product markets, the expansion of international trade and capital flows, the skill-bias of recent technological advances, and changes in the organisation of firms – have led to an increasing dispersion of wages or employment opportunities in many OECD countries. This dispersion has been amplified through the asymmetric course of policy retrenchment since the 1980s. As transfers to the middle classes have remained intact while support for the poor and disadvantaged has fallen away, the distribution of economic outcomes has inevitably widened further. Thus societies have become progressively polarised, between the long-term employed and the long-term unemployed, the high-wage and low-wage earners, or those with abundant and favourable job opportunities and those with few and unfavourable ones. As firms become increasingly vulnerable to market forces, there is a danger that long-term commitments between employers and employees may become increasingly unstuck, thereby reducing the incentives to invest in training. Social polarisation threatens the efficiency of market transactions by encouraging crime and necessitating rising expenditures on crime prevention.

THE "QUICKSAND EFFECT"

In retrospect it can be seen that, just as many of the common OECD policy systems amplified the favourable social and economic developments of the 1950s and 60s, so they are amplifying the unfavourable developments that have occurred since then. This could be called the "quicksand effect". It signifies that, in the long run, the prevailing policy systems have not provided a firm foundation for supporting people against poverty and uncertainty and promoting prosperity and social cohesion. Rather, the more people need to be supported, the greater are the political and economic pressures on governments to reduce that support. The prevailing systems, in other words, are a bit like quicksand: they start giving way as soon as enough weight is placed on them.

Conversely, the less support is required, the greater are the political pressures to make it more generous. This is the sense in which the prevailing policy systems have created economic and social imbalance over the long run.

A GENERAL STRATEGY OF POLICY REFORM

It is important to keep in mind that this imbalance is the product of past policy decisions, which may be revised once the source of the imbalance has been recognised. To find the appropriate guidelines for policy reform, European governments must first understand the need to design policies that are automatic stabilizers in two senses at the same time: when there is increased likelihood of an adverse economic or social contingency – such as the risk of unemployment, illness, poverty, insufficient education and training opportunities, insufficient support for old age – the policies must automatically provide:

- more support for the people affected by that contingency; and

- greater economic incentives to overcome the contingency.

How would this strategy apply to, say, the reform of unemployment policy? The aim would be to replace current measures by ones that have the following dual stabilizer function: when unemployment rises, they must automatically provide *i)* more support for the unemployed and *ii)* greater incentives for employment creation and job search.

Current unemployment benefit systems fulfil the first condition but not the second. When unemployment rises, the government's aggregate unemployment benefit payments increase, providing more support for the unemployed. But incentives for employment creation and job search are reduced: unemployment benefits discourage the unemployed from seeking jobs, for when they find a job the benefits are withdrawn and taxes are imposed. Furthermore, unemployment benefits discourage employment by putting upward pressure on wages. And because current unemployment benefit systems do not act as unemployment stabilizers in the second sense, the quicksand effect arises. In augmenting the underlying unemployment problem, these systems destabilize the government's budget and thereby create political pressures to make such systems less generous.

Reform should be aimed at breaking this trade-off between stability of people's incomes and stability of the government budget deficits. Before examining the requisite reform strategy, it is useful to consider some important recent developments that may be expected to make the underlying problem worse – and thus the need for reform more urgent – with the passage of time.

CHALLENGES TO SOCIAL COHESION

There are a number of important challenges that will make it increasingly difficult for policy-makers to achieve prosperity growth *together with* social cohesion in the decades ahead. Although these challenges are strongly interrelated, they will be considered under the broad headings of *a)* globalisation and skill-biased technological change, and *b)* changes in the organisation of firms.

Globalisation and skill-biased technological change

In recent years it has often been claimed that the gradual erosion of barriers to international trade and foreign direct investment has expanded both market opportunities and the competitive pressures faced by many companies in the OECD countries, and that this has created an increasingly global matrix of business strategies. One important consequence, so the story goes, is that the advanced market economies are achieving an ever more pronounced comparative advantage in the production of commodities that are relatively intensive in skilled labour.[1] This is often touted as the reason why the demand for skilled labour has risen relative to that for unskilled labour in Europe as well as the United States.[2]

The response in the United States, where wages are comparatively flexible, has allegedly been increasing wage dispersion; in many European countries – where wages are compressed through legislation, centralised bargaining, norms, union pressures, and welfare state entitlements – the result has been rising unemployment of unskilled people. In either case, the resulting trend toward greater inequality in income and wealth is seen to pose a major threat to social cohesion in the advanced market economies. It is also viewed as endangering the future prosperity of these countries, as goods requiring low-skill labour inputs are increasingly imported and factories to produce these goods are increasingly shifted to the low-wage economies of the Far East and Central Europe.

This account doubtlessly has some explanatory power, but it does not tell the full story since it does not fit all the relevant facts:

– Trade flows are probably still too small a proportion of national product in Europe and the United States to account for more than a small percentage of the massive increase in European unemployment and the dramatic fanning out of American wage distribution over the 1980s.

– A significant amount of trade between the advanced market economies of Europe and the United States (on the one hand) and the emerging markets of Asia and the East (on the other) is intra-industry – not inter-industry – trade, even at the three-digit level; and there is little reason, of course, why intra-industry trade should raise the demand for skilled relative to unskilled labour.

– According to conventional wisdom,[3] the expansion of international trade induces the unskilled workers to move from the import-competing sectors (where wages are comparatively low and/or unemployment is comparatively high) to the protected sectors. But there appears to have been little movement of this sort in the advanced market economies. Instead of a change in the industry mix – a rise in the use of skilled labour in the sectors producing skill-intensive goods and a fall in the use of labour elsewhere – most sectors have increased their ratio of skilled to unskilled labour.

– It is far from clear that the skill level (weighted by population) of the countries trading with Europe and the United States has, on average, gone down (on account of, say, the increasing role of China in world trade) or up (on account of the rising skill levels of, say, the Japanese and Korean workforces).

Beyond that, technological change is often deemed to be another explanation for the joint problems of increasing wage dispersion and unemployment in many OECD countries. It is argued that technological change over the past two decades has been heavily skill-biased – once again, raising the demand for skilled relative to unskilled labour.[4] There is some evidence that firms spending relatively large amounts on R&D tend to pay relatively high wages to their skilled employees.[5] There is also evidence that workers who use computers tend to earn relatively high wages.[6]

There is, however, an important sense in which this is not an explanation at all. Economists define technological change as anything that shifts the production function. It is the residual change in output, after all other sources – namely, change in the use of inputs – have been accounted for. Since it is a residual, where it comes from is simply not known. Thus, to say that the rise in demand for skilled relative to unskilled workers is due to skill-biased technological change is virtually like saying it is not known why this change in relative demand has occurred.

In any case, it is clear that globalisation and skill-biased technological change are bound to make many of the current economic policy systems greater sources of imbalance. The reason is that, by widening the distribution of incomes, they widen and deepen citizens' reliance on public support and thereby augment the quicksand effect.

The organisational revolution

Another important development, documented extensively in the recent business management and sociological literature[7] but largely ignored by the economics profession,[8] is a constellation of phenomena that could be called facets of the "organisational revolution". It has the following salient features.

First, in a significant and growing cross-section of companies in the advanced market economies, the command-and-control style of management – where authority flows from the senior executives down through middle management to the workers in the functional departments – is being replaced by a flatter organisational structure, with a large number of teams reporting directly to the central management with few, if any, intermediaries.

In the process, the functional specialisation of the traditional firms is being reversed: each of the small teams performs many of the separate tasks that used to be divided among separate departments. The teams are now often organised with reference to particular sets of customers rather than tasks. It is the "integration" of tasks that permits the teams to give customers more individual attention. This development also means that substantial layers of middle management are no longer needed.

Second, there are radical, interrelated changes in the organisation of production. In both the manufacturing and service sectors, returns to scale in production are drastically reduced with the introduction of flexible machine tools and programmable equipment and the use of computer-aided customisation of goods and services. Setup and retooling costs have come down, which permits production in smaller batch sizes, shorter production cycles, smaller delivery lags, and – with the help of computer-aided design – quicker product development.

These changes have enabled producers to adopt ideas such as "lean production" (keeping inventories low) and "just-in-time production" (delivering supplies only when they are required). These are not simply cost-cutting devices; together they constitute a method of decentralising the production and associated learning processes, since they expose bottlenecks where they arise and give the front-line workers the opportunity to overcome them on their own. The new innovations also permit an increasing degree of integration between design, engineering and manufacturing.

Third, there have been dramatic changes in the nature of products and in seller-customer relations. The new "holistic" companies offer broader product lines in smaller quantities. There is also greater emphasis on product quality and sensitivity to purchasers' requirements: products are developed and improved over progressively shorter periods of time, methods of quality control are becoming steadily more stringent, and more product adjustments are made in response to customer demand. There is also increasing scope for customer participation in the design of new products. These include not only information and repairs, but also prompt processing of orders and individualised marketing.

Fourth, in the new types of business organisations, occupational barriers are beginning to break down, as employees are given multiple responsibilities, often spanning production, development, finance, accounting, administration, training and customer relations.

The new, smaller, customer-oriented teams require versatility and cognitive and social competence, as well as judgement. What matters is not simply the competence in a particular activity of production, organisation, development and marketing, but rather all-round knowledge, the potential to acquire multiple skills, and the ability to learn how the experience gained from one skill enhances another skill. In this context, traditional occupational distinctions begin to lose their significance and what is meant by "skilled" versus "unskilled" workers radically changes.

The implications of these developments are far-reaching. To begin with, they help explain the rising resistance to centralised wage bargaining relative to firm-level bargaining in many OECD countries. A standard objective of centralised bargaining is "equal pay for equal work", and thus it invariably imposes some uniformity of wages across workers for given tasks. But when employees are given multiple responsibilities, spanning various complementary tasks, this practice can become very inefficient, for there is no reason to believe that the productivity of one employee's time at a particular task should be similar to the productivity of another employee's time at that task. For instance, there is no reason that time spent with customers should affect the productivity of a product designer in the same way that it affects the productivity of a production worker. Thus the restructured firms often have an incentive to offer different workers different wages for the same task. But that is precisely the practice that centralised wage bargaining inhibits. In this way, the restructuring process raises the efficiency costs of centralised bargaining and thus gives employers and employees growing incentives to choose decentralised bargaining arrangements instead. This, however, may be expected to increase wage dispersion in countries where centralised bargaining has compressed the distribution of wages.

Furthermore, insofar as women tend to specialise less in terms of skills than men, these developments help explain some of the narrowing male-female wage differentials and nonemployment differentials. And finally, insofar as people within given occupational, educational and job tenure groups differ substantially in terms of their versatility as well as the social and cognitive skills necessary for success in holistic organisations, these developments also offer a new explanation for the widening wage dispersion *within* such groups.

The organisational revolution magnifies the influence of globalisation and skill-biased technological change on the performance of the currently dominant OECD policy systems. Specifically, the organisational revolution makes it more likely that these systems will become a source of economic and social imbalance in the long run. The reason is that, by increasing the dispersion of incomes between versatile and non-versatile workers and between well educated and poorly educated ones, and by making jobs less secure, this phenomenon is likely to create greater social reliance on unemployment insurance, public support for education and training, and a wide variety of welfare state services. The process greatly increases the risk of generating the quicksand effect.

ILLUSTRATIVE REFORM PROPOSALS

To meet the challenges above, many OECD countries require a fundamental reform of their current policy systems, so as to avoid the pitfall of relying on measures that give way as soon as there is a significant demand for them. As noted, a promising way to do so is to design networks of policies that not only give automatic support to people facing adverse economic and social contingencies, but also automatically provide greater economic incentives to overcome these contingencies. The following complementary policy approaches are a good illustration of how this could be achieved.

The Opt-Out Programme

The idea behind this proposal[9] is simple. To begin with, everyone in the economy is classified by income, age, sex, marital status, and other major determinants of people's demand for welfare state services, and a computation is made of the per capita cost of these services within each group. The proposal is then to give people the option of relinquishing their entitlements to these services in specific areas in return for a rebate amounting to x per cent of the cost of the services within their particular group. (In practice, the rebate could amount to about 70 per cent.)

If the entitlements accrue at the present time (as in the case of public education for people with children of school age), the rebate would take the form of a tax reduction. If, on the other hand, the entitlements are to accrue in the future (as in the case of pensions for those of working age), the rebate would take the form of a bond, with a maturity commensurate with the time when the entitlements accrue. This option is to be supplemented by compulsory insurance against sickness, disability and old age.

That would leave (1 − x) per cent of the funds to cover the deadweight loss arising when people who consume a disproportionately small fraction of each type of service take disproportionately large advantage of the opt-out option. By specifying the personal characteristics of each opt-out group sufficiently narrowly, governments could reduce the deadweight loss to below x per cent of the available funds, leaving a surplus to improve the state-provided services.

The motivation is to put the decision between public and private welfare provision into the hands of the consumer. The failure of central planning to bring living standards in Eastern Europe and the former Soviet Union into line with those in advanced market economies indicates how important it is to get this decision right. The strength of the advanced market economies has been to put the decision into the hands of the consumer. The Opt-Out Programme puts the division of responsibility over welfare state services into the consumer's hands as well.

It is often argued that allowing people to leave the welfare state system would turn it into a poverty programme, and that services for the poor eventually turn into poor services. This argument, however, does not apply to the Opt-Out Programme. First, there would be no special incentive for the rich to opt out while the poor stay in. Those affluent people who consume little of these services would get a small rebate and have a correspondingly small incentive to opt out. Those making greater claims on these services (such as the middle classes on pensions and education, or the poor on housing and non-contributory benefits) would receive a larger rebate and have a correspondingly larger incentive to opt out. Second, under the Programme, the size of the rebate for those who have opted out is tied to the cost of the state-provided services for those who have remained in. Thus, those who opt out would have no incentive to vote for a run-down of the state sector.

The Opt-Out Programme is equivalent to giving everyone a voucher for specific welfare state services, with the size of the voucher depending on personal characteristics, and somewhat larger vouchers going to those who do not opt out of the state system. The Programme thereby gives people appropriate incentives for choosing between public and private provision of welfare state services. People who opt out will be the ones whose particular needs can be met more adequately through private providers. Given the enormous diversity of needs and the inevitable standardization of publicly provided services, it is inevitable that such people should exist. Consequently, the public and private welfare state systems would exist side by side, each providing services in which they have a comparative advantage. The resulting competition would give both systems an incentive to become more efficient than they would otherwise be.

In short, the Opt-Out Programme is a straightforward way for governments to reduce their spending on the "welfare society" without putting significant segments of the voting population at a disadvantage. The reduction in distortionary tax-and-transfer arrangements should gradually generate enough saving for the government – through taxation of the new private sector welfare provision – to permit improved state provision.

Operating as a dual stabilizer, this Programme avoids the quicksand effect. It not only provides support against economic and social uncertainties, but also automatically raises the incentives to overcome these uncertainties when the need of support increases. Under the policy regime established by the Programme, a government that reduces its welfare state services in the face of budgetary pressures would thereby induce more people to opt out of public sector provision. Since these people would all receive rebates for relinquishing their entitlements to public support, this policy strategy would not ease the government's budgetary problems; the government would be forced to internalise some important social costs and benefits of its welfare state involvement.

Government loan guarantees

This proposal involves a simple, inexpensive way in which the government could help the private sector to provide some important welfare state services more efficiently.

Many of the problems that the welfare state attempts to address have their origins in imperfect capital markets. The problem of unemployment is an example. The hardship from unemployment is due not only to the reduction in people's lifetime income but also to their inability to borrow against their incomes in future periods of employment. The most appropriate way of dealing with this problem is not through government provision of unemployment benefits, but through government loan guarantees.[10]

The reason why the free market generally does not give people the opportunity to borrow against their human capital is that banks usually have trouble collecting the debts from people who change jobs and geographical regions; lending on the basis of human capital would thus encourage default. The government, however, has a comparative advantage in this area. Unlike banks, it is able to trace people through the tax system and is thus in an advantageous position to make loan guarantees. Once loans on human capital have thereby been made possible, people's unemployment durations would become more efficient since they would now come closer to paying for the cost of their unemployment as well as receiving the benefits from a judicious job match.

Roughly the same approach is also appropriate to education. The main reason why the free market provides less than the efficient amount of education is that students are generally unable to borrow against their future incomes. Government loan guarantees would help students, particularly poor students, in acquiring a more efficient amount of education, since they would come closer to internalising both the costs of and benefits from their education.

Loan guarantees for health insurance would also promote efficiency in this market and help bring poor people's opportunities for health cover a step closer to those of the more affluent.

This policy clearly has a dual stabilizer function that helps circumvent the quicksand effect. The loan guarantees would be maximally effective in providing support against unemployment, education and health care when the public's need for these services was greatest. Since the loan guarantees would stimulate private sector activity, the government's tax revenue from this activity may generally be expected to outweigh its costs of loan default, thereby making the government's budget less, rather than more, sensitive to external shocks.

Support accounts

This proposal is to replace current public support systems by *support accounts* (SAs). The budgets of the current public support systems – such as unemployment benefit systems, public pension plans, nationalised health care and publicly provided education – are often financed out of general taxes. Under this proposal, employed people would be required to make ongoing contributions to their SAs and the balances on these accounts would each be used to cover their pension requirements, their health and education needs and their income support whenever periods of unemployment, illness or disability lead to financial distress.[11]

The basic idea is to replace the current tax-and-transfer system – whereby general tax revenues are used to finance unemployment benefits, pensions, public health and education – by a system of compulsory private saving. When people become old, unemployed, ill, disabled, or have children of school age, their with-drawals from their SAs would substitute for the unemployment benefits, public pensions, etc. they currently receive. Thus their financial support would depend significantly on the accumulated balances in their SAs.

To meet its equity objectives, the government would top up the contributions of individuals in the lowest income groups. In fact, when an individual's SA has been exhausted (i.e. the SA balance falls to zero) and all permissible transfers among SAs have been exploited, the person would become entitled to assistance from the government on precisely the same terms as those under the current public support systems. Correspondingly, a portion of each employed person's SA contributions would be spent month by month on an "assistance charge" to help finance that assistance.

When people's SA balances are sufficiently high, they could use the surplus funds for any other purposes; and at the end of their working lives, their remaining SA balances in their unemployment accounts could be transferred into their pension schemes. Balances remaining at the end of one's life could be bequeathed to one's successors.

The aim of the proposal is to reduce the major efficiency losses created by the current public support systems without sacrificing their underlying redistributive goals. For example, unlike unemployment benefits, the unemployment SAs would do less to discourage job search, for when unemployed people find a job and contribute to their unemployment SA, they are reducing the financial uncertainty associated with future periods of unemployment, and creating wealth that they will be able to use later on. Moreover, the pension SAs would do less to discourage saving than public pension plans, since pension SA balances can be bequeathed whereas the public pension plans cannot.

People would be given some discretion over who could manage their SA funds: the government or financial institutions in the private sector. To minimise the danger of bankruptcy, the financial activities of the private-sector SA fund managers would have to be regulated, along lines similar to the regulation of commercial banks.

The process of transition from the current public support systems to ones based on SAs would of course have to be gradual. It takes time for people to accumulate the requisite SA balances. Perhaps the simplest way of organising the transition process would be to put new entrants to the labour force under the SA system. The Opt-Out Programme would enable people to speed up this transition process, perhaps substantially.

It is easy to see that the SAs would act as automatic stabilizers in both senses above, not only securing people against uncertainties and stabilizing their incomes, but also creating greater incentives to overcome the underlying problem. Unemployment SAs, for example, would not only provide support when people are unemployed, but also generate greater incentives for employment creation and job search as unemployment rises. The greater the expected duration of unemployment, the greater would be the incentive for people to avoid periods of unemployment – for the longer a person is unemployed, the lower would be their unemployment SA balance and thus the fewer the funds available to them at a later date. In this way, the unemployed person would internalise many of the social costs generated by their unemployment.[12] And this efficiency gain could be achieved without sacrificing underlying redistributive goals. Besides, the unemployment SAs are more efficient than unemployment benefits at redistributing income from rich to poor, since unemployment benefits are not targeted at the poor whereas government unemployment assistance under the SA system is.

Moving from the current public support systems to the SA system could have a profound effect on economic activities. People would have greater incentives to avoid the risks of unemployment, illness and disability. The reason is that under the current systems, there are few financial penalties. For example, people pay no costs for remaining unemployed other than those associated with current income forgone and a possible reduction in prospects of future employment. When an unemployed person finds a job, his unemployment benefits and various welfare state entitlements are withdrawn and taxes are imposed, and this discourages him from job searching. The disincentive effect is particularly large for people considering the move from unemployment into part-time or temporary employment. Under the SA system, by contrast, this disincentive effect would be far less pronounced.

On this account, the SA contributions necessary to finance a particular level of unemployment, health, and disability support (in the form of SA disbursements) will be lower than the taxes necessary to finance the same level of support under the current system of public provision financed through general taxation. In this way, the public stands to gain from a switch from the current public support systems to the SA system.

Conditional negative income taxes

The previous proposals mainly had to do with promoting prosperity by making the provision of state services more efficient. The paper now examines proposals primarily aimed at promoting social cohesion through the redistribution of income. On the whole, most OECD countries conduct such redistribution in exceedingly inefficient ways, needlessly reducing incentives for employment and production and imposing unnecessary burdens on governments' budgets, thereby enhancing the quicksand effect.

This section considers a promising, largely untried policy alternative: the conditional negative income tax. To put the advantages of this policy into sharp perspective and to illustrate what the negative income tax should be "conditional" on, it is useful to view it as replacing a current redistributive policy, such as the unemployment benefit system. In this context, the conditions attached to the proposed negative income tax would be analogous to those attached to current unemployment benefits. For instance, if, under the current unemployment benefit system, people must provide evidence of serious job search in order to qualify for benefits, then they must also be required to provide such evidence under the proposed conditional negative income tax system. If unemployment benefits decline with unemployment duration under the current benefit system, then so too must the negative income taxes.

The broad argument in favour of a switch to negative income taxes is that this policy could meet the equity and efficiency objectives of current unemployment benefit systems more effectively than the unemployment benefit systems themselves. Although conditional negative income taxes would generate the same type of policy inefficiencies, they would tend to do so to a lesser degree. For example, negative income taxes may be expected to discourage job search but by less than unemployment benefits, for when a worker finds a job he loses *all* his unemployment benefits, but only a *fraction* of his negative income taxes.

It is worth noting that a major criticism of the traditional negative income tax schemes – namely, that they make people's material well-being less dependent on employment and thereby discourage employment – obviously does not apply to *conditional* negative income taxes, since these taxes are conditional on the same things as current unemployment benefits.

Furthermore, conditional negative income taxes tend to be more effective in overcoming labour market inefficiencies generated by credit constraints (*e.g.* the inability to take enough time to find an appropriate job match or to acquire the appropriate amount of training), since the presence of these constraints is more closely associated with low incomes than with unemployment.

Against this, conditional negative income taxes are by nature less effective than the economic theorists' socially optimal unemployment insurance schemes in overcoming efficiency problems in the unemployment insurance market (such as the problems of moral hazard and adverse selection). The reason, of course, is that conditional negative income taxes are designed to reduce people's risk of poverty rather than of unemployment. However, the practical significance of comparing conditional negative income taxes with socially optimal unemployment insurance schemes is generally small, since the unemployment benefit systems operative in most OECD countries do not have much in common with the central features of optimal unemployment insurance. One reason is that most of the existing unemployment schemes either impose ceilings on benefits or offer these benefits as flat rates, while optimal unemployment insurance does not have this property. In many European countries, the duration of unemployment benefits is not closely tied to the previous span of employment, clearly not the case with optimal unemployment insurance. Moreover, the relative contributions of employers, employees and the government to the current unemployment insurance schemes bear little if any relation to the social costs that these agents fail to internalise.

Given that unemployment benefit systems in practice have little in common with the main features of optimal unemployment insurance, the efficiency case for the former is considerably weakened. What remains, then, is the equity case; but here, as noted earlier, unemployment benefits tend to be less effective than conditional negative income taxes.

Finally, the unemployment benefit system has a well-known advantage: since it is more narrowly targeted than a conditional negative income tax system which provides a similar level of support for the target group, it tends to be less expensive. Specifically, the unemployment benefit system requires a lower level of tax revenue to finance a given level of support for its target group. This disadvantage of conditional negative income taxes versus unemployment benefits must be set against the advantages noted above. Should the disadvantage prove to be overwhelming in particular instances, policy-makers may wish to target the conditional negative income taxes in the same way as the unemployment benefits are currently targeted.

The Benefit Transfer Programme

As rising unemployment represents one of the severest challenges to the achievement of prosperity and social cohesion in many OECD countries for the twenty-first century, it is of paramount importance to consider how policy inefficiencies and inequities in this area can be undone. The aim of the Benefit Transfer Programme[13] (BTP) is simply to redirect the funds that the government currently spends on the unemployed – in the form of unemployment benefits, temporary lay-off pay, redundancy subsidies, poverty allowances, etc. – so as to give firms an incentive to employ these people.

The BTP would give the long-term unemployed the opportunity to transform some of their unemployment support money into vouchers that could be offered to firms that hire them – the longer people are unemployed, the greater the value of the vouchers that employers would receive for hiring them. Employers would also be given a higher voucher amount if they could prove they were using them entirely to train their new recruits.

If the unemployment support came in the form of benefits, the BTP would enable the long-term unemployed to transfer a portion of these benefits into employment vouchers. If, on the other hand, the support took the form of unemployment SA balances, the BTP would permit the long-term unemployed to offer a fraction of these balances as an inducement to potential employers.

The BTP would be voluntary, and so would extend the range of choices open to the unemployed and their potential employers. The unemployed will join only if it is to their advantage. Many could become much better off, since the wages they would be offered could be significantly higher than their unemployment benefits. At the same time, employers will join only if they find it profitable. Once again, many could well do so, since the vouchers could significantly reduce their labour costs. In short, employees may wind up receiving substantially more than their unemployment support, and many employers may find themselves paying substantially less than the prevailing wages.

The BTP would be an automatic stabilizer in both senses above. As unemployment rises, the aggregate amount of funds available for unemployment support would rise (because more people are drawing on their unemployment benefits or their SA balances) and thus more funds would automatically be available for employment vouchers. Thus, in the process of stabilizing incomes, the Programme would simultaneously provide incentives for employment creation and job search when they are needed most.

Beyond that, the BTP would clearly not be inflationary, since *a)* it would reduce firms' labour costs and *b)* the long-term unemployed have no noticeable effect on wage inflation. It would cost the government nothing, since the money for the employment vouchers would have been spent on unemployment support anyway. By offering higher vouchers for training, the Programme could become the basis for an effective national training initiative. Clearly, firms will spend the vouchers on training only if they intend to retain their recruits after the subsidies have run out; thus the training for the unemployed would automatically come with the prospect of long-term employment. This is something that the existing government training schemes do not offer. Many such schemes also run the risk of being ill-suited to people's diverse potential job opportunities, whereas under the BTP firms would provide the training most appropriate to the available jobs. And whereas existing training schemes are costly to run, the BTP is free.

Finally, the BTP could play a vital role in tackling regional unemployment problems. Regions of high unemployment would become areas containing a high proportion of workers with training vouchers, thereby providing an incentive for companies to move there and provide the appropriate training.

The fall in unemployment would also give some governments the opportunity to expand their tax base by raising the retirement age for both men and women to 70. The cost of social provision to the taxpayer has exploded, not just because these services have been getting steadily more expensive but also because many governments artificially depress the number of taxpayers through its retirement legislation. People not only live longer than they used to; they continue to be productive longer. By putting many elderly people out of work long before they cease being productive, governments increase the number of dependants on the welfare state and reduce the number of persons providing financial support. Raising the retirement age would keep advanced industrialised countries from hamstringing themselves in this curious way.

CONCLUDING THOUGHTS

The reform proposals above are all part of a single, coherent strategy that is meant to promote prosperity and social cohesion by reversing the long-run instability inherent in many of the dominant policy systems in OECD countries. The paper has argued that such reform is particularly important nowadays, since OECD Member countries face some rapidly growing challenges to social cohesion in the years ahead: globalisation, skill-biased technological change, changes in the organisation of firms, and lagging productivity growth in the welfare state sector. What these developments have in common is that they all tend to yield greater dispersion of both wages and employment opportunities within the advanced market economies of the OECD, so that a given amount of economic prosperity can be achieved only through social polarisation and loss of social cohesion. These developments imply a growing need for a social safety net and for insurance against economic uncertainties – a growing need, in other words, for welfare state services. But as productivity growth in the welfare state sector continues to trail behind average productivity, the cost of welfare state services will continue to rise, and the need for these services will become ever more difficult to satisfy. Progressive dismantling of the prevailing policy systems will, over the long run, amplify unfavourable economic and social shocks and thereby impart an imbalance to their host countries.

The paper has also suggested that, to avoid this "quicksand effect", OECD countries require a new generation of policy systems that have a "dual stabilizer" role: when adverse economic or social contingencies arise, these systems must automatically provide both support for those affected *and* greater economic incentives to overcome such contingencies. The five reform proposals above – the Opt-Out Programme, the government loan guarantees, the Support Accounts, conditional negative income taxes and the Benefit Transfer Programme – are illustrative of this fundamental reform strategy. They all serve to give individuals greater responsibility and greater choice in the provision of public goods. In addition, they provide people with greater incentives to avoid wasting resources in the production and distribution of these goods.

They rest on the realisation that some of the major market failures in OECD countries are the outcome of existing public policies, since these policies often distort individuals' incentives to achieve their economic goals efficiently. The reform proposals aim to readjust these incentives by helping individuals internalise the main costs and benefits of their activities. Although the need for social cohesion makes a total internalisation of these costs and benefits socially undesirable, it is clear that many of the prevailing redistributive policies are needlessly inefficient. The reform proposals above point to a strategy for achieving redistributive goals at minimal efficiency cost. They may thereby provide a vital opportunity of achieving prosperity together with social cohesion in the twenty-first century.

NOTES

1. See, for example, Leamer (1994), Sachs and Shatz (1994), and Wood (1994).

2. In accordance with the Stolper-Samuelson theorem, the fall in demand for unskilled workers will spill over from the tradeable to the non-tradeable sectors.

3. This view is founded on the Hecksher-Ohlin theory of international trade.

4. See, for example, Bound and Johnson (1992) and Mincer (1989, 1991).

5. For example, Machin (1996).

6. This is documented in Berman, Bound and Griliches (1993) and Krueger (1993). Krueger claims that computer use on the job can account for $1/3$ to $1/2$ of the rise in the rate of return to education.

7. For a survey of the evidence on these developments, see Appelbaum and Bott (1994), Hammer and Champy (1993), Lundgren (1994), Pfeffer (1994), and Wickström and Norman (1994).

8. A first attempt to subject these phenomena to economic analysis is made in Lindbeck and Snower (1995a, b) and Snower (1996d). Milgrom and Roberts (1990) examine a subset of these phenomena relevant to manufacturing.

9. For a rigorous analysis, see Snower (1996b).

10. See Snower (1993).

11. This proposal is similar in spirit to the Central Provident Fund system in Singapore. It bears some resemblance to the reform proposal in Folster (1994). For an analytical study, see Snower (1996c).

12. Some of the disincentive effect remains, of course, through government unemployment assistance and the associated charge.

13. For a more detailed analysis, see Snower (1994).

BIBLIOGRAPHY

APPELBAUM, Eileen and Rosemary BOTT (1994), *The American Workplace*, ILR Press, Ithaca, New York.

BERMAN, Ely, John BOUND and Zvi GRILICHES (1993), "Changes in the Demand for Skilled Labor with US Manufacturing Industries: Evidence from the Annual Survey of Manufacturing", NBER Working Paper No. 4255.

BOUND, John and George JOHNSON (1992), "Changes in the Structure of Wages in the 1980s: An Evaluation of Alternative Explanations", *American Economic Review*, June, pp. 371-392.

FOLSTER, Stefan (1994), "Social Insurance Based on Personal Saving Accounts", mimeo.

HAMMER, Michael and Kames CHAMPY (1993), *Re-engineering the Corporations*, Harper Business, New York.

KRUEGER, Alan (1993), "How Computers have Changed the Wage Structure: Evidence from Microdata", *Quarterly Journal of Economics*, 108, pp. 33-60.

LEAMER, Edward E. (1994), "Trade, Wages and Revolving Door Ideas", NBER Working Paper No. 4716.

LINDBECK, Assar and Dennis J. SNOWER (1995a), "Restructuring Production and Work", Discussion Paper, Department of Economics, Birkbeck College, University of London.

LINDBECK, Assar and Dennis J. SNOWER (1995b), "The Reorganization of Firms and Inequality", forthcoming in the *American Economic Review, Papers and Proceedings*.

LUNDGREN, Hakan (1994), *Sacred Cows and the Future: On the Change of System in the Labour Market*, SAF (Swedish Employers' Confederation).

MACHIN, Stephen (1996), "Changes in the Relative Demand for Skills" in Alison Booth and Dennis J. Snower (eds.), *Acquiring Skills*, Cambridge University Press, pp. 127-146.

MILGROM, Paul and John ROBERTS (1990), "The Economics of Modern Manufacturing: Technology, Strategy and Organization", *American Economic Review*, pp. 511-528.

MINCER, Jacob (1989), "Human Capital Responses to Technical Change", NBER Working Paper No. 3207.

MINCER, Jacob (1991), "Human Capital, Technology, and the Wage Structure: What Do the Time Series Show?", NBER Working Paper No. 3581.

PFEFFER, Jeffrey (1994), *Competitive Advantage through People*, Harvard Business School Press, Boston, Mass.

SACHS, Jeffrey D. and Howard J. SHATZ (1994), "Trade and Jobs in US Manufacturing", *Brookings Papers on Economic Activity*, 1, pp. 1-84.

SNOWER, Dennis J. (1993), "The Future of the Welfare State", *Economic Journal*, 103, pp. 700-717.

SNOWER, Dennis J. (1994), "Converting Unemployment Benefits into Employment Subsidies", *American Economic Review, Papers and Proceedings,* 84(2), pp. 65-70.

SNOWER, Dennis J. (1996a), "The Low-Skill, Bad Job Trap" in Alison Booth and Dennis J. Snower (eds.), *Acquiring Skills*, Cambridge University Press, pp. 109-124.

SNOWER, Dennis J. (1996b), "Restructuring the Welfare State", Discussion Paper, Department of Economics, Birkbeck College, University of London.

SNOWER, Dennis J. (1996c), "Unemployment Support Accounts", Discussion Paper, Department of Economics, Birkbeck College, University of London.

SNOWER, Dennis J. (1996d), "Centralized Bargaining, Unemployment, and the Organizational Revolution", Discussion Paper, Department of Economics, Birkbeck College, University of London.

WICKSTRÖM, Solveig and Richard NORMAN (1994), *Knowledge and Value*, Routledge, London.

WOOD, Adrian (1994), *North-South Trade, Employment and Inequality: Changing Fortunes in a Skill-Driven World*, Clarendon Press, Oxford.

4

A LIBERAL SOCIO-ECONOMIC SCENARIO FOR THE EARLY TWENTY-FIRST CENTURY

by
Henri Lepage
Délégué Général
Institut Euro 92

The following conjectures aim at presenting the outlines of a liberal socio-economic scenario for the coming two decades. The exercise implies sticking to rough features, even if this entails a risk of oversimplification. But that is the rule of the game.

A NEW MONETARY SYSTEM

Starting in the late 1970s (after the abolition of Regulation Q, which kept a watertight separation between the American money market and the international eurodollar market), financial globalisation has become a major event. However, one may ask whether all the consequences of globalisation are always fully understood. This is especially true regarding its impact on the international monetary system.

With the generalised use of hedging mechanisms (stock options, derivatives, etc.), almost surreptitiously, and through a process of spontaneous order, central banks and governments have lost a great deal of their freedom to print money. Indeed, it is as though through these new instruments lenders had at last found an insurance tool which enables them to keep interest rates at the level which suits them best.

The time of monetary illusion and plunder through the printing press is up. With the increasing sophistication of monetary and financial instruments, lenders and money-holders now have access to tools which enable the markets to sanction instantly those countries that are financially negligent. Governments printing too much money will immediately find inflation expectations being capitalised in rising interest rates. Those who believe they can inflate will find themselves creating deflation through prohibitive interest rates.

The development of futures markets all over the world gives rise to a new and totally unexpected situation, with central banks discovering they can no longer rely on their seignorage power. This may sound exaggerated, but it sums up a strong impression shared by an increasing number of economic observers:

– It would seem that, without noticing it, we have put into place a new international monetary system. We have entered the age of a "Futures Exchange Standard" that makes any long-term flight into inflation impossible; at last, governments are forced to keep their promises.[1]

– We have returned to a kind of new gold standard, but without gold: a new monetary system whose monetary and economic constraints are even more severe – more "deflationary" – than those of the gold standard, since it leaves no more room even for the "inflationary" safety-valve of gold discoveries!

A WORLD WITHOUT INFLATION

It follows from the above that:

1. The disinflation that the world economy has experienced since the early 1980s has not yet reached the end of its course.

2. The end of inflation is a worldwide trend that will continue to determine our economic environment for at least ten to fifteen years.

3. This phasing-out of inflation is a long-term process whose origin lies in a complex and dynamic chain of "deflationary" forces that have been active for about ten years, but which should continue to make their effects felt well beyond the beginning of the twenty-first century.

After thirty years of a trend towards ever-increasing inflation rates, we are now entering – if not permanently, at least for some time – a world without inflation. One consequence is that interest rates will stay at historically high levels for years to come ("historically high" meaning levels on average higher than economic growth rates).[2]

GOVERNMENTS ON A DIET

For public opinions, the 1980s were above all the years when mass unemployment was discovered. Joblessness hit people from every social class, following an upward curve which nothing seemed able to hold back.

The causes of mass unemployment are known. It is mainly the result of economic and institutional rigidities hampering markets, especially labour markets. Its explosive increase stems less from sluggish economic growth rates than from an increasing sclerosis of our welfare state institutions. This is happening at the very moment when more flexibility is warranted, because Western economies are being exposed to ever more intense competition (emerging Asian economies, achievement of the European single market, more than two billion additional potential producers following the end of the cold war, and a technological revolution that brings new incentives to delocalisation and changes in production patterns, drastically reduces production costs, and spawns radically new activities whose development destroys the old cartels).[3]

Some countries understood the nature of this new challenge more than others. But most preferred to put their head in the sand. Hiding behind temporary scapegoats – the OPEC cartel countries, for instance – their leaders thought it could only be a transitory crisis, as it had always been in the past. As monetary tools were no longer available (because of disinflation), they chose to wait for the famous Keynesian "stabilizers" (increased deficit spending and traditional budget policies) to restore economic growth and thus solve the unemployment problem.

The result has been exploding public expenditures with deficits, skyrocketing government debt, and rising taxes. But when interest rates are higher than the growth rate, debt quickly turns into a snowball effect where interest payments increase more rapidly than government income. Furthermore, since rising taxes demotivate people, hamper entrepreneurship and job creation, and in the end quash growth, government finances are soon caught in a trap: debt is piling up even faster.

In just six years, global debt of G7 countries has gone from 50 to 73 per cent of GDP. With the likely evolution of interest rates, but also the prospect of still stronger international competition, such a development is no longer sustainable. The world has thus entered a new era where major industrial countries are no longer allowed to let their budgetary deficit grow significantly. Since the option of letting inflation eat up the debt is no longer available, the only way out is public spending deflation; some countries already have a head start in the new venture (the United Kingdom and New Zealand, for example), but most have only just begun.

This public consolidation of finances will progressively lay the ground for a new period of economic growth. But it will not be a politically easy task. Politicians will have to overcome many obstacles: achieving a real (and not only nominal) reduction in public spending, redefining government functions, contracting the number of civil servants and reviewing the level of benefits and the structures of welfare institutions, as well as overseeing a complete audit of social legislation, radical deregulation, privatisation and breakup of state utility monopolies (telecoms, electricity, railways, mail service...), tax reform, etc.

The progressive fall in interest rates, decreasing taxation and a return to a greater flexibility of markets will ultimately yield a genuine supply shock to countries which are furthest ahead in this process. But in spite of European constraints – most notably the "fast forward" push to respect the EMU timetable – this will take time. Ten years seems reasonable; it took almost fifteen for Britons to begin enjoying the benefits of Thatcherite policies.

THE CLASSICAL BUSINESS CYCLE REAPPEARS

Governments have two traditional tools for gearing the economy: 1) interest rates and monetary policy; 2) public expenditure and budgetary policy. In the 1980s, with the globalisation of financial markets, they lost control of the first. Since the beginning of the 1990s, they have been losing control of the second. The consequence: a deep change in the nature of economic cycles. Economists ought to change their frames of reference and ways of thinking.

Since the Second World War and the Keynesian revolution, governments have managed activity and employment levels by adjusting public spending and the money supply. The result was inflationary growth with a business cycle dominated by credit and consumption variations, and a cycle time frame that was closely set by political events (especially the American presidential elections, with their regular four-year cycle).

With government influence increasingly on the wane, one must expect the classical business cycle – where growth is led by investment, entrepreneurial action and industrial innovation – to take over and set a new tempo for the economy.

This is what occurred in the nineteenth century. Growth was linked to novelties, discoveries: developing new territories, inventing new products, investing in a new technology. The "entrepreneur" pulled the economy along. Increasing purchasing power and consumption were only the end result of a process which started with a rise in profitability, went on with strongly increased investment expenditure, and led to job creation and therefore to a higher purchasing capacity for the population at large. Recessions originated in overinvestment which created overproduction, a fall in sales and prices, bankruptcy for small producers and decreased investments, which in turn led to more unemployment and then falling demand. This process usually took ten years on average – six to seven years for the boom and three or four for the bust (Juglar cycle).

Considering the early 90s recessions (United States, Sweden, Japan, France), it is clear that this model – where financial variables and debt levels are the leading elements – provides a much better fit to what actually took place than the traditional politico-economic explanatory models of the past. One may wonder whether what we are experiencing is not a return, after 75 years, to a world close to that which the West knew before the First World War, one in which capitalism comes back to its old deflationary roots. A world of "deflationary growth" based on innovation, savings, investment and distribution of productivity gains through a long trend of a slight average fall in prices (according to productivity gains). A world which would very much look like the one imposed on us by gold standard economics, and which today would be the end result of our new "Futures Exchange Standard" financial constraints.

A NEW PRICE ENVIRONMENT

Should this hypothesis be confirmed, a most important conclusion will have to be drawn: negative inflation rates – *i.e.* a real fall in nominal prices – is something that may happen again. Drops in prices will not necessarily be very large, as in times of depression. But we may expect a new price environment with up and down movements around a long-term trend of slightly falling prices.

Until the First World War, this was the rule of Western industrialised economies. During the nineteenth century, prices went down more often than up (on average, two years out of three). Deflation was the rule of the time, so much so that in 1910 the American price index was back at its 1790 level, before the great inflation of the Napoleonic wars. Contrary to what is usually believed, one can no longer exclude the possibility of returning to a price environment of this kind.

Economists generally do not believe it. Thanks to progress in economics and monetary science, most people think that we have the technical and institutional means of avoiding such a setback. Is it not the duty of central banks to maintain stable prices in the face of both rising and falling price trends? Hence the incredulous attitude towards the prospect of returning to a world of falling prices.

Can we be sure of this? Not so long ago, the very same experts were nurturing the illusion that it was possible to encourage growth indefinitely by stabilizing inflation at a "reasonable level" of a couple of per cent.[4] They had thus discovered the "magic concoction" of modern economics! Alas, this was not the case. The desired stability was but theoretical. From one step to the other, inflation started growing more rapidly until its vicious circle became unsustainable. Neither the progress of economics nor the panoply of central banks' increasingly sophisticated monetary models could stop it.

Does anyone think that the task will be easier when it comes to "stabilizing" inflation at zero rather than at 5 or 6 per cent? Why should zero inflation be more enchanting? The general price level is but an abstraction, the synthesis of a multitude of relative prices. Even if it is possible to observe an empirical *ex post* relationship between currency and price series (the quantitative monetary theory), it is the indirect result of a million local Brownian fluctuations.

In order to attain a fixed price level (in this case zero inflation), central banks would have to accumulate knowledge on relative productivity changes all over the economy, and be able to compute what monetary compensations need to be given locally in order to obtain a stable price index. This amounts to a planning task which is as presumptuous and impossible as that of the Soviet Gosplan, for the same basic reasons as the ones expressed before the Second World War by Professor Hayek in his now-famous controversy with Oskar Lange and all the leading economists of his time. The odds of a central bank getting it right are about the same as for finding a needle in a haystack. And nothing warrants the claim that the risk of erring downwards is necessarily smaller than erring upwards. This is even more true since long-term disinflation modifies behaviours, and reduces confidence in the predicting power of traditional monetary equations.[5]

THE END OF MONETARY ILLUSION

Many people will dismiss such a view as pure fantasy. It attacks a dogma which nobody is yet prepared to question openly, *i.e.* that of nominal wage rigidity.

Falling prices imply that wages also move up and down. That may have been the case in the nineteenth century, when no organised and powerful trade union yet existed. But to imagine that such a thing could return seems unrealistic to most. Even if disinflation made it possible to break the upward wage/price spiral by stabilizing the rise of real wages (adjusted for inflation), who would agree to a reduction of their nominal wage? There are two responses.

The first focuses on monetary illusion. Disinflation was made possible because economic agents became vastly more sophisticated economic men. Keynesian economic management proved efficient as long as governments were able to cheat, *i.e.* to create false expectations. The inability of individuals to anticipate fully the real results of government decisions maintained the illusion that the latter had indeed the capacity to push or restrain economic activity at will.

As time passed, this illusion gradually evaporated. If governments currently feel that the economy is getting beyond their control, if the levers of money supply and public expenditure are increasingly ineffective, this is not only because markets are getting larger and competition stronger. It is also, and above all, because the majority of economic agents are now able to anticipate precisely the final results of public policy decisions. The monetary illusion does not exist any more.

Using the nominal wage rigidity argument would mean that wage earners are the only economic agents incapable of distinguishing between a nominal and a real purchasing power increase. That is to say, those who have proved their ability to understand that inflation is a zero-sum game when nominal wages are increasing less rapidly than the price index would suddenly lose their use of basic arithmetic as soon as prices start to fall. They would not be able to realise that with nominal wages remaining constant their purchasing power still increases. Such an argument betrays a lack of consideration for the dignity of the common man. Why would economic agents, who are capable of perfect anticipation in the financial markets, behave differently as simple wage-earners? Why would they turn out to be more impervious to new information than anyone else?

True, there is the problem of allowing time for adjustment. But it seems reasonable to assume that working people are human beings who are at least as able as anyone else to adapt their behaviour to a world of stable prices, or even to one of falling prices.

CHANGING VALUES

The second reason has to do with the change in attitudes and values that is bound to occur if the hypothesis of a deflationary economic environment is confirmed. It particularly relates to changing attitudes in the field of employment and labour organisation. Eighteen years ago, under the sponsorship of the Institut de l'Entreprise, this author published a book explaining that defending free market institutions was not incompatible with a desire to have our societies evolve toward new values and production systems allowing less materialistic and more "convivial" human relationships.[6] The aim was to reply to self-management leftist enthusiasts to whom capitalism necessarily was an obstacle on the road to promoting more convivial social structures allowing more intense, more personalised and more enriching individual relationships. It was hoped to show that:

1. The tools of economic analysis – taking into account the "cost of time" – are just as capable of explaining how non-market behaviours evolve as they are of explaining market relationships.

2. A competitive market economy – provided it remains protected from government – is as likely to adapt to a higher demand of relational values as it is to marketable values.

3. There is no irreducible one-way relationship between capitalism and heteronomy (a concept that comes from the writings of Ivan Illich, the leftist intellectual guru of those times, which describes the crushing of individuals by industrial mega-systems).

The book concluded by defending the idea that through recent developments in information technology (microprocessors, electronic communication, meganetworks...), the world was on the brink of another great technological revolution that, in toppling the structure of contemporary society "information costs", would reinforce the evolution of relative social costs and prices in favour of more autonomous and more "convivial" ways of doing things.

Eighteen years later, many elements of the book are still utopian.

Nevertheless, the technological revolution is here, and deflation – which sharpens competition everywhere – is a powerful factor which accelerates its process.

THE JOB-SHIFT

Kondratieff cycle long-term economic history reminds us that "deflationary" phases usually go along with spectacular technological jumps. It is during these periods that long "waves" of technological innovations occur, as Schumpeter described them.[7]

The reason is not that inventors and innovators are more numerous, or more active in some periods than others. It simply has to do with the fact that deflationary periods, because of their economic and financial environment of high interest rates and wider growth in industrially emerging countries, are more favourable to large-scale aggressive innovation developments. These are periods when entrepreneurs are more than ever led to intensify the introduction of new production techniques and new work methods.

The disinflation trend following the change in the early 1980s is no exception to this rule.

It should come as no surprise that books about "the end of the workplace" have multiplied for some time. This is not a reference to works such as Jeremy Rifkin's about job destruction and the need for a co-ordinated rationing of working hours – but rather, analyses such as William Bridges'. According to Bridges, the best specialist on contemporary changes in the workplace, we are facing the end of wage-earning activities as we know them – *i.e.* the emergence of new working arrangements leading to a greater degree of individual working autonomy and the phasing out of traditional long-term one-company job contracts.[8] Bridges believes that lifetime employment, permanent employment, protective status, wages automatically predetermined by detailed collective agreement schemes, fixed working periods and working hours will all soon be part of history. Flexible working hours, adaptable management, individualised salaries, performance-related pay, zigzag careers, permanent professional training and retraining, new forms of self-employment: these will all eventually erase the present distinction between the organisation – the "employer" – and the individual – "the employee".

The work environment will more and more resemble a galaxy in which a multitude of "Me Inc." companies and "You & Co." firms will gravitate around a few big-name corporations, reduced to the size of a nucleus of top managers. Large corporations will shrink to retain a hard core of employees and work with a very large number of outside autonomous professionals who will no longer be full-time wage earners. "It is not work as such that will disappear but employment. The work will have to be done otherwise than by employees on long-term contracts".[9]

If this prospect is confirmed, structural wage rigidity will be considerably reduced. It will be like the economists' dream come true: part of work-related remuneration will adjust flexibly up and down all along the business cycle phases. That will be the end of the main endogenous source of unemployment: labour as a resource whose price does not adjust to market forces because of unions' cartel power.

From a macroeconomic point of view, we will definitely have moved into "a new world". A world where the general price level will follow productivity, and where purchasing power gains will come less from individual salary increases than from falling prices of goods and services.

NINETEENTH CENTURY TEACHINGS

What about growth? In people's minds, but also economists', deflation has a bad reputation. The very idea of deflation is automatically linked to that of depression. Typical is the definition of deflation given by French journalists during the debate of the summer of 1996, a debate sparked by politicians: "a general fall in production, prices and incomes".[10] In fact, strictly speaking, deflation means "falling prices" and nothing but that.

Is there necessarily a connection implying that deflation automatically brings depression? Is growth possible only in an environment where prices go up? Why should it be incompatible with a long-term fall in prices?

If we consider price movements on the one hand and growth on the other, four scenarios are possible: positive inflationary growth (inflationary growth); negative growth with falling prices (deflationary depression); negative growth with rising prices (stagflation); and positive growth with falling prices (deflationary growth).

Theory as well as economic experience since the beginning of the industrial age (roughly since the early nineteenth century) shows that, in the long term, there is no link between price evolution and economic activity. Any of the four scenarios is possible.[11] The dominance of one or the other originates in the long-term institutional arrangements on which depends the economic and monetary regulatory framework, which is itself always evolving.

Economic history of the nineteenth century (in fact, until 1914) confirms that in the long run the inflationary or deflationary nature of price movements is independent from average long-term economic performance.

Examination of two curves – one showing the consumer price index in the United States from 1860 to the present, the other showing the change in the industrial production index over the same period – clearly reveals that the United States has gone through long periods of deflation. From 1867, just after the Civil War, to 1897 – for thirty years – prices went down almost all the time. The same trend may be observed from 1921 to 1934 (thirteen years). Prices had already fallen continuously from 1810 to 1830, and from 1830 to 1860 they remained at a quasi-stable level. It follows that in the nineteenth century, and until 1940 – with the exception of the First World War – prices fell more often than they rose. The same curves show that this predominantly deflationary price system did not have much of an impact on the progress of American industrial production. It is true that the 1930s' massive deflation ended up in the Depression. But conversely, the United States experienced an enormous deflation from 1868 to 1898, and still managed to increase industrial production considerably. From 1860 to 1914, prices in the United States sometimes rose, sometimes fell, without showing any clear and unequivocal relationship with production. There were periods of depression when the country registered falling prices and a fall in production. But these periods were definitely less numerous (by far) than those with increasing production and falling prices (periods of deflationary growth).

These data are relevant for the United States. They show that during deflation, economic activity may be either expanding or contracting, but it does not mean that structural secular production increases are stopped. The same results appear in the British, French or Belgian data presented in Professor Dupriez's book. Germany is the only exception (experiencing at the time an inflationary growth typical of an emergent country catching up with the development of others).

The message is clear. If history is any guide, there is no reason to see the end of inflation as a calamity. Nothing in the change of our global monetary environment warrants doomsday speeches on "the end of economic growth".

FROM INFLATIONARY GROWTH TO DEFLATIONARY GROWTH

It is true that, in a first period, such a change necessarily implies negative consequences for growth, for three reasons.

The first relates to delays in adjusting behaviours and expectations. When new and more restrictive, perhaps even deflationary, monetary policies are brought in, it takes time before everyone adapts to the new situation. Everyone expects prices to go up faster than they do. Economic agents find themselves with less cash and liquid assets than they would want. In order to raise cash, they sell their assets and lower their prices, thus exercising a recessive pressure on economic activity – pressure which, beyond short-term cyclical variations, remains as long as individual expectations have not entirely adjusted.

The second has to do with fallout effects of "economic globalisation". The enlargement of growth opportunities in the world means that the cost of making economic choices goes up.[12] One now has to be informed about a greater number of competing markets. Moreover, the prospects of new companies entering into competition on these markets are enormous. Thus it becomes increasingly difficult to discriminate between "good" and "bad" investment opportunities in companies, sectors or entire regions. The risk of making mistakes likewise increases. The result is a greater spread of financial performances among Western firms, and thus greater uncertainty concerning future income rises. This in turn means a less elastic response in consumption or investment to a fall in interest rates. Other things being equal, a stronger movement in rates is needed to get the same reaction from consumers and investors. Business cycle models built on regressions of the past systematically "overestimate" – or "overanticipate" – the economy's capacity to bounce back.

Thirdly, increased socialisation and increased taxes brought about by the public finance sector plight carry depressive economic consequences.

However, these are transient factors. As private expectations adjust to new monetary policies, and as privatisation, demonopolisation, deregulation, government reforms and tax cut policies move along, there is no reason to believe that within the next ten to fifteen years Western economies will not progressively return to average growth rates more in tune with their secular trend.

Some will get back on track faster than others. Others will be late or in danger of slipping definitively backwards (as Argentina did in the 1930s). But globally the analysis is clear – even if our hypothesis of a long-term deflationist environment is correct.[13]

THE WELFARE STATE BOWS OUT

Economic growth will return; but it will not be a return to *status quo ante*. For in the meantime deflation will have claimed at least one victim: the welfare state. What will replace it? How will our societies manage to preserve their social cohesion if the main institutions on which they rested are challenged? The decline of the welfare state, as we have known it since the war, cannot be checked. The proximate cause, *i.e.* the crisis in government finances, is not the only one. There are three additional fundamental reasons.

1) *The welfare state is an "unsustainable" institution.*[14] It is easy to understand why such a system was created. Welfare and solidarity ideas of the late nineteenth century certainly played a great part. But a more decisive step was the two world wars. Financing this European civil war was done in the very same way French revolutionaries financed their war against the rest of Europe: savings of past generations were expropriated through inflation.

With savings gone, swallowed up in this conflict, something new had to be invented to ensure old age security. The only available option was a transfer system, financed through levies on the working generation – redistribution – banking on the hope that the debt thus acquired by the younger generations for their efforts in favour of their older parents would similarly be repaid by the following generations. And so on. This system was hailed as a progress of "civilisation", *i.e.* a social model which would endure over generations. What we then failed to see was that, by design, this system was not "sustainable". It is a system which, by definition, could have but a transitional value, while waiting for the reconstruction of a genuine international system of savings.[15] Why? Because such a system inevitably leads to the destruction of the demographic mechanism needed to ensure its perpetual restart.[16]

The problem lies in the consequences of generalised socialised insurance for the future of family structures and for birth rates. Socialising welfare destroyed the demographic balance of industrialised countries by depriving the family of one of its basic tasks: catering to the needs of older generations.

2) *This system of socialised care has lost its moral and financial legitimacy.* Ten years ago, an economist from New Zealand, David Thomson, showed how the focus of welfare continuously changed. In the beginning, it concentrated most of its transfers on family and housing needs of young couples. In other words, transfers basically benefited the generation which had come of age at the end of the war. The official reason was of course to protect all citizens against risks of various kinds. But the truth is that most government expenses went to the young adults then entering their professional life. Then a curious thing happened: the focus changed, and not in any haphazard way. It followed the changing needs of this particular generation. Since the 1970s, retirement benefits, old age assistance, health care (largely concentrated on the elderly) and disability benefits have become the heaviest part of the transfer system, whereas transfers to younger generations are constantly shrinking.

Hence David Thomson's conclusion: the welfare state, under the cover of great humanitarian considerations, is a concept which used to serve the interests of just a few generations – those who took part in the building of the system – at the expense of those who came afterwards. "We have created", Thomson explains, "a two-speed Welfare State: not that of the middle class versus that of the poor as is often believed; but those who contributed a little and gained a lot more versus those who pay a lot and will get much less".[17]

In this context, what happens to the principles which are the cornerstones of the social pact on which our welfare state rests: equality, reciprocity and solidarity? Does anyone think that younger generations will remain eternally loyal to the institutions which their parents bequeathed to them, first and foremost for their own sake?

3) *Changes in the working environment will make traditional social security arrangements obsolete.* Social security is indeed based on the notion of employment. Being employed is what gives a person the right to welfare benefits. The cost of protection is assessed on wages. The entire philosophy of socialised welfare is linked to the era of industrial mass organisation and a stable job culture. What is the point of such a system once employment withers away and most employees turn into self-employed individuals? How can it go on working in a "post-wage" environment where holding a fixed job ceases to be our normal condition? The next

twenty years will obviously bring about considerable changes in the way of looking at, thinking about, and organising protection against risks and hazards. It is an entire culture – one long- and heavily conditioned by inflation – that will have to change.

A NEW RELATIONSHIP WITH TIME AND SAVINGS

It is much too early to determine the exact outline of these transformations. However, the main vectors may already be perceived. The first will no doubt be a transition to more individualised security systems, relying on subsidiarity principles for their management. We already know their main outlines through reforms introduced in some countries where implementation is more advanced (new Dutch pension and insurance schemes, reform plans in Germany, more radical examples in Chile and New Zealand).

The next ten years will probably witness the introduction of clearer distinctions between what relates to insurance (financed by individuals) and what should remain within the realm of solidarity (tax-funded). By pretending that everything should be financed in common, the link – present in the insurance business – was cut between each individual's efforts and the costs and benefits which he or she gets from them. Also, excessive concentration and bureaucratisation were favoured by the assistance systems. The goal of social policy over the next ten to twenty years will be to reverse these tendencies.

Governments will increasingly stop doing directly what may be delegated to regional, municipal, co-operative, mutualist or private organisations which will compete on an open market for medical insurance, retirement benefits, work accidents, and also unemployment insurance. On the other hand, government schemes will most likely keep taking care of long-term unemployment, congenital handicaps, basic pensions and old age assistance, as well as providing a minimal health insurance.

The increasing gap between employment and work, the development of composite careers and the multitude of companies for which everyone will be working during their professional lives will naturally lead a growing number to choose personalised and privatised ways of covering their risks (pension funds).

This evolution will be doubly favoured by the change of price system (deflation) and by the dynamics of financial globalisation. By reversing the economic agents' relationship to time, deflation will provide powerful stimuli for the larger private savings needed.

It will also be favoured by the changing role of trade unions. Due to long-term changes occurring in the workplace, they will develop consulting activities away from their mass organisation traditions, and evolve as a kind of professional community, closer to a medieval guild or a modern private interest defence association.

Rethinking the role of trade unions will also help reduce political and intellectual opposition to the restructuring of current social systems.

THE REVIVAL OF CIVIL SOCIETY

The second major tendency will be the rise of new ideas and values (an ideology) favouring the birth and spread of intermediary organisations which belong neither to the restricted circle of family or clan solidarity, nor to that of mass industrial movements.

The perverse consequences of "centralised solidarity" are becoming clearer to all. In spite of the gargantuan sums which are claimed by these systems, they are constantly proving their inability to deal with problems of poverty and marginalisation for which they were – in theory – created. Hence the revival of "communitarian" ideals aiming at letting citizens themselves – and no longer cold and distant burcaucracies – devise "neighbourhood" solutions for everything pertaining to education, the fight against poverty, exclusion, drug trades, taking care of the young, dynamising a local environment, etc.[18]

This resurrection of civil society will be more active in countries that already have a strong tradition of "broader communitarian sociability" (the Anglo-Saxon countries). But as Francis Fukuyama underlines in his latest book, even the other countries will have to catch up fast as adaptability and flexibility, and therefore confidence (trust), will more than ever constitute the great virtues needed for economic success in the new global universe of hypercomplexity and Global Village.[19] To the author of *The End of History*, this implies the comeback of a number of "pre-modern" values – the notions of moral obligation, duty toward community, reciprocity – which are the source of trust needed for creating a spirit of community belonging, whether the latter is anchored in the love for a given territory or expressed through abstract networks of fraternal relations via a space like Internet.

Modern technology itself is a factor helping in the revival of civil society. It squashes the cost of time, of information, of communication, while "conviviality" and communitarian activities rely heavily on those inputs. Finally, the end of steady employment positions as well as the surge of "telecommuniting" will thus gain a new opportunity. Everyone will at the same time be more involved in their own "neighbourhood" community and be a member of nationwide or worldwide networks, which will allow more experience-sharing.

Therefore, in large part due to the specificities of our new technological systems and their demands upon us, the future would lie in restoring values and social cohesion systems usually described as "conservative".

THE COMEBACK OF CONSERVATIVE VIRTUES

This last remark brings us back to deflation, since price systems are never ethically neutral.

As early as 1944, in *The Road to Serfdom*, responding to Keynes's economic ideas, F.A. Hayek already perceived what were going to be the moral consequences of inflation: here-and-now choices displacing forward-looking decisions, consumption being favoured over savings, acting like parasites rather than responsible individuals, favouring redistribution lobbies rather than personal foresight, making cheating more profitable than hard work, etc.

Return to a stable price system – or a slightly deflationist one – will most likely lead to an opposite ethical revolution.

In an inflationary universe, the demand for "social justice" could only be satisfied through redistributive political procedures. As inflation left little space for individuals to provide for long-term contingencies – due to the continuous plunder which resulted from arbitrary price increases and prevented individuals from making long-term plans – redistribution through the creation of what Jacques Rueff called "paper rights" (*faux droits*) was inevitable.

Equal opportunity was then achieved through redistribution, massive public investment in education, and "democratisation" of real estate speculation.

In a stable, non-inflationary world, or even a world of controlled deflation, things should be very different. First, there would be a more symmetrical situation for debtors and creditors. Inflation plunders creditors and favours a transfer in real terms towards the debtors. Deflation favours creditors who hold fixed incomes and whose purchasing power increases with falling prices, but – to the extent that deflation sticks to the margin of productivity gains – it is not followed by a worsened situation for debtors whose fixed obligations increase but whose real income increases also. The same goes for the non-working generation (the retired). In an inflationary environment, those without a salary only benefit from productivity gains to the extent that their retirement benefits are revalued. This usually occurs with some delay, and allows a certain politicisation of decision-making (the winners being those who belong to the most efficiently organised professions or pressure groups).

"DIFFERENT ETHICS"

In a world where the general price level follows productivity gains, distribution of these gains will happen not through a rise in wages, but through the fall of commodity prices – which makes it accessible equally and immediately not only to those who hold a job but also to those who do not.

That distribution of productivity gains will of course be unequal, according to sectors, activities, relative performance and rising or declining professions. People will not be equal. However, a world without inflation is a world which reduces the importance of this issue by being more favourable to individual accumulation (and therefore to individual foresight), as well as by reducing obstacles to mobility. It is a world where the value of property is safe; as long as the fall in prices does not exceed productivity gains, investments and property keep their real value.[20] It is thus a universe where one may safely plan again for the long term.

It is, finally, a universe where honouring one's word is also again a virtue. It is a universe which maximises liberty by founding it on keeping one's contracts and promises, and thus on a return to the basic values of a society founded on the rule of law and individual rights. It is not so obvious that such a world may be morally inferior to the world of inflation we have known since the end of the war. It is, at any rate, one of "different ethics".

NOTES

1. For developments of this idea, see Charles Gave, *Les conséquences économiques de la Paix (avec nos excuses à John Maynard Keynes)*, Cursitor-Cecogest (Stratégie Internationale d'Investissement), Paris, June 1996.

2. Three reasons – to which the paper returns – support this analysis. First, the revolution of so-called "emerging countries", which does not yet appear to have exhausted all its effects: the higher investment yields in this part of the world form a floor for world rates. Second, the public finance crisis in Western countries, which leans heavily on market rates; it is not unrealistic to think that ten more years will elapse before it is cleared out. Third, the prospect of bankruptcy facing the current welfare states. As that prospect becomes more obvious to everyone, populations feel the need to complement the existing institutions by accumulating personal savings. In the long term, this will cause interest rates to decrease as individual savings are rebuilt and adapted to hedging techniques. But that will not happen overnight.

3. See the study by Giles Keating, Chief Economist at CS First Boston: "Will Disinflation End?", a speech given at the Euromoney International Bond Conference, London, 14 September 1995. His thesis is that the very features of the current technological revolution reinforce the dominance of anti-inflationary behaviours. Irruption of new technologies accentuates the uncertainty of economic choices, but leads individuals to accept it because of the enormous gains involved. For individuals, luck is more important than ever, but stakes are also higher. Such a situation is not prone to cartel strategies, whereas the opposite was true in the preceding period. This situation should last until new activities reach their technological maturity. The period following will see the return of cartel-forming strategies aimed at "closing" markets for the benefit of those who were first to get a place in the sun. According to Keating, this should not occur before another ten years.

4. This is an illusion which is again fashionable due to recent writings by Professors Krugman and Akerlof. Under a threshold of 4 per cent, the cost of disinflation in terms of employment and unemployment would steadily increase. See the study by George A. Akerlof, William T. Dickens and George L. Perry, *The Macroeconomics of Low Inflation*, published by the Brookings Institution, Washington, DC, 1996.

5. There is also the argument that contemporary disinflation successes are a proof of central bank efficiency. In fact they are a phenomenon which, without questioning the competence of people involved, may be explained much more by the pressure of

economic and institutional mechanisms taking place within the framework of long-term economic fluctuations than by the wisdom, will-power and knowledge of some eminent civil servants.

6. See Henri Lepage, *Autogestion et Capitalisme: Réponses à l'Anti-économie*, Masson-Institut de l'Entreprise, 1978, especially Part 4, "L'utopie capitaliste".

7. See the famous work by Professor André Dupriez of Louvain University: *Des Mouvements Economiques Généraux*, Nauwelaerts, 2 volumes, 1951. In the early 1980s, the Kondratieff cycles were fashionable again as people were becoming conscious of technological changes and the imperatives of industrial restructuring they entail (Christian Stoffaës, *La Grande Menace Industrielle* (Revised), Le Livre de Poche, Collection Pluriel, 1979). But most economists who refer to the Kondratieff cycle adopt the Schumpeterian explanation of its origins (the phenomenon of "clusters" of innovations). The current thinking is that these technological phenomena are in fact endogenous to economic long-term trends.

8. William Bridges, *Jobshift*, Addison Wesley Publications, 1994.

9. See in *Le Nouvel Economiste*, No. 1066, 31 October 1996 the interview with William Bridges by Bernard Lalanne. High-tech sectors (telecoms, electronics, multimedia), Bridges explains, are already spearheading the change. The transition may be completed in less than a decade, but it will take perhaps fifty years in the heavy and slow industries where competition is less stiff.

10. Laurent Mauduit in *Le Monde*, 12 October 1996.

11. On this subject, see the dossier "Ce que dit la théorie économique" in *Valeurs Actuelles*, 21 September 1996, in particular the article by Pascal Salin, "Les mécanismes de la déflation. Inflation, déflation, croissance et dépression: les définitions et le rôle de la monnaie".

12. It should be stressed that the enlargement of the world economy through the integration of new production zones entering global trade is also a phenomenon typical of long-term "deflationary" phases. Those familiar with Kondratieff cycle theory know that each downturn phase is accompanied by the arrival of new countries within the club of developed economies. This extension of the international market area is one of the strong features of "downturn" phases of the cycle. As paradoxical as it may seem, it is not during "upward" turns that the phenomenon of spatial catching up occurs.

13. The same goes for the danger of "deflationary depressions". It is true that such risks exist. But as we have seen in the early 1990s, these are greatest in the beginning of the period as long as the nature of the new monetary order has not been clearly evaluated. They then pertain above all to a pathology of accidents created by political errors, generally linked to a mismanagement of interest rates. Further, these risks are even more real if the economic agents of the country are highly indebted, if restoration of government finances is lagging, and if citizens are desperately hanging on to the handouts distributed at the time of inflationary growth.

14. The concept of sustainability is used here in analogy with the notion of "sustainable development".

15. The present trend of "global finance" may be conceived of as a process leading to the restoration of a worldwide savings-mobilising structure, anticipating the death of the welfare state.

16. On this subject, see Bertrand Lemennicier, "Retraites: l'arithmétique de la transition", Institut Euro 92, March 1996.

17. David Thomson, "Generations, Justice and the Future of Collective Action", a paper written for the Conference on the Relations between Generations, Austin, Texas, 20-22 October 1988.

18. On this topic, see the excellent survey on the welfare state published by *Critical Review*, Volume 4, Number 4, Autumn 1990.

19. Francis Fukuyama, *Trust: The Social Virtues and the Creation of Prosperity,* Hamish Hamilton, London, 1995.

20. What will guarantee that deflation will stay within these limits? This is once more the problem of macroeconomic monetary regulation. At the beginning of the century, classical economists defended the idea that "deflation" should be the normal long-term price system in a developed economy. It is what would naturally occur within a monetary system without a central bank, resting on competing "private" currencies. In a central bank system, they claimed, the role of the latter should be to aim at a goal of macroeconomic stability of the national nominal income, rather than stabilizing the general price level. In their view, such a rule of economic and monetary management would be more just and moral in the sense that it restores a greater symmetry between creditors and debtors. But it also would be easier to implement, because this type of management would enable public authorities to attain their goals by economising on local relative price adjustments – which would reduce the risks of microeconomic maladjustments, and thus minimise the probabilities of uncontrolled macroeconomic slippages compared to the alternative of a system of zero inflation. That is why, according to the American economist George Selgin, author of a bestselling book on free banking and the history of competitive currencies, such a system of "normally falling prices" would typically be "more sustainable" in the long term, and would thus reduce the instability of real economic variables (production, employment). In other words, from a purely technical point of view, a rule of "slightly falling prices" following productivity gains would be easier and socially less costly to manage than a zero inflation goal.

5

TOWARDS A NEW EQUILIBRIUM OF CITIZENS' RIGHTS AND ECONOMIC RESOURCES?

by
Claus Offe
Institute for Social Sciences
Humboldt University of Berlin

All societies, in order to reproduce themselves in a manner compatible with the notion of "social order", must solve two reciprocal core problems in institutionalised ways. First, they must allocate (adult) human labour power to valued ("productive") functions, thereby situating "people" into "places". The set of allocation rules through which this task is performed includes selective exemptions from the expectation to perform economically valued activities that apply, in our society, to the young, the old, the sick, and the independently wealthy. Putting people in places is a process that results in patterns of (however unequal) inclusion, participation, recognition, self-respect, and discipline, as well as an overall pattern of division of labour. It provides people with relatively stable expectations as to where they belong and what conduct is appropriate in work and in life. Second, societies must provide people, in equally patterned and routinised ways, with the means of livelihood in return for the valued functions they perform (or have performed at earlier points) and as a precondition of the continued performance of these functions. These means include income (or the claim to means of the consumption of "goods") and protection (or the, at least partial, compensation of risks, or the incidence of "bads").

These two problems – the problem of production and the problem of distribution – can be institutionally solved in a myriad of ways. They vary among societies and historical epochs, and across institutional sectors. Slaves and serfs, soldiers and monks, students and peasants, workers and housewives partake in some patterned way in the socio-economic equivalent of specific duties and rights which together make up (on an individual level) their social identity, as well as (on a collective level) the social order. In modern societies, the principal institutional pattern governing both valued activities and the individuals' share in the outcomes of production is the labour contract, to be entered into voluntarily by demander and supplier and, at least as an ever-present possibility, unilaterally terminated by either of these actors. Most other patterns of production and reproduction, such as those applying to children, retired people, homemakers, the sick or recipients of charity, are normally considered to be in preparation for, subordinate to, or derivative from the key mechanism of paid employment, if not conditional upon the recognised exemption from the general expectation of paid or otherwise gainful employment. If people are fully employed, at least some of the necessary condition of the realisation of values such as freedom, prosperity, efficiency and justice are thought to be fulfilled.

But the centrality of the labour contract as the foundation of social order shows signs of erosion. Or rather, it continues to be counted upon as central, but it fails to perform its function as the cornerstone of allocation and distribution and hence (by implication) of social order.

The "problem of unemployment" comes to mind as the most obvious demonstration of this failure of the key institutional pattern of contractual labour. But measured unemployment is a misleading, euphemistic – at best, incomplete – indicator, as it systematically underestimates the actual extent to which the institutional pattern of the labour contract and the labour market fail. This institutional failure takes many forms, some visible, some not so obvious. In order to capture conceptually the entire range of relevant phenomena, one is tempted to rely on awkward conceptual neologisms such as "precariousness of social situation" and "precariousness of subsistence", *precariousness* in both cases connoting shakiness and harmful unpredictability, as well as the lack of social recognition and appreciation that is associated with this condition. In short, the labour contract fails both to assign a "place" in society to increasing numbers of people, and to provide those people with adequate income and protection.

Precariousness of situation is a condition of "non-regular" employment that affects a wide variety of people. Beyond those registered and counted as "unemployed", the category would cover all "discouraged" workers – that is, persons who work part-time but are willing and able to work full-time; it would also include workers who, more or less voluntarily, make the transition to early retirement or who, for equally ambiguous motives, undergo various forms of training. Quasi-self-employment and fixed-term employment are further cases in point.

With regard to precariousness of subsistence, it is important to note that there is no one-to-one relationship to the former category. One can be involuntarily "out of work" and still enjoy a decent standard of living and protection (*e.g.* due to the presence of family support and workable arrangements of social welfare and assistance); and, more importantly in the present context, one can inversely be fully integrated into some kind of productive process without enjoying a level of subsistence and protection considered adequate according to prevailing standards within a society – the phenomenon of the "working poor" in the United States or, in Europe, the "unprotected" workers whose income remains below the level that would make them eligible for social security benefits in return for mandatory contributions.

This dual precariousness, and the crumbling of the labour contract and full employment paradigm as the cornerstone of social order, form the topic of the present paper. Various causal factors are assessed (Section 1), consequences are described at least in broad outlines (Section 2), and the choice of policy responses and proposals are explored and evaluated in terms of criteria of justice as well as effectiveness (Section 3). A tentative policy proposal, together with a scenario of economic conditions, social conflict, and the configuration of political forces, will conclude the discussion (Section 4).

1. CAUSAL INTERPRETATIONS AND ASSOCIATED REMEDIES

Explanations of high and persistent levels of precariousness pinpoint a bewildering variety of causal factors: technological, microeconomic, macroeconomic, political, institutional and socio-cultural.

Technological explanations of un- and underemployment point to the disparity encountered by typical OECD economies between the growth rate of labour productivity, at least in the manufacturing sector, and the growth rate of economic output. As labour becomes more productive, and the effect is not offset by sufficiently steep rates of overall growth of output, the result is a vast underutilisation of the labour supply. At the same time, chances to reduce unemployment to anything deemed "normal" through the acceleration of economic growth must be considered plainly unrealistic, as an (already ambitious) growth rate of 2.5 per cent is needed in order to keep registered unemployment from further increasing. The same verdict of totally unrealistic applies to the other side of the growth-productivity relation. If growth cannot be increased by political means, can labour productivity be made to increase more slowly? The answer is a plain "No", the reason being that a strategy that would forgo potential productivity gains would be punished by international competition.[1] For the bitter truth is that unemployment is the result of the market-enforced behaviour of both the winners and the losers in the competitive game, as the shedding of labour through the introduction of labour-saving technical change is the prerequisite of competitive survival as much as it is the consequence of competitive failure.

To frame the same idea of productivity vs. growth differently, we can also speak of technical change being biased in favour of process innovations and against product innovation, fuzzy though the demarcation line often is between the two (as illustrated by the case of the personal computer). Putting the question in these terms invites the subsequent question: what kind of new products, and in what volume, could conceivably meet with effective consumer market demand (and at the same time cause relevant labour market demand) in the rich OECD economies? There is no easy answer to this question, unless an answer is imagined in terms of goods that are not being marketed, but which rely on "forced consumption" (such as defence goods, or highway construction, or devices for air and water pollution control) paid for out of the state budget. If anything, speculating about what sort of goods large numbers of people would be willing to buy in considerable quantities might well bring the answer: the goods that we know already (e.g. cars), only with a longer life expectancy, or duration of use. If this is the answer, it is bad news in the context of our problem (in spite of its considerable attractiveness in terms of "green" political values). For in the long run, it would lower (instead of increase) the demand for new goods, as technical obsolescence and the need for replacements would manifest themselves less often per unit of time.

The offshoot of this kind of technological argument is usually that there remains in fact one kind of goods for which there is claimed to be both a virtually unlimited demand and a very limited potential for labour-saving process innovation – namely services. However, in spite of the hardly disputable societal "need" for services, there are basically three kinds of economic "bad news" associated with this vision of a society of post-industrial service employment. First, many service activities (such as design and accounting) are directly tied to production, so that a relative decline in the growth rate of production affects the demand for these services as well. Second, the price at which (e.g. medical) services are supplied reflects directly their lesser availability for technical efficiency increases (although service productivity increases are by no means to be ruled out, as a glance at the technological revolution in banking services reveals). The rate of increase of service prices surpasses that of the secondary sector, with or without the additional impact of (particularly public) service sector unionisation. Third, the demand for most services is known to be highly price-elastic, with the implication that the perform-ance of paid services tends to be substituted by unpaid self-service,[2] be it due to suppliers' or consumers' initiatives. These considerations add up to the assessment that the restoration of full employment is not to be anticipated within the frame-work of an emerging "service society" and that an exception to this rule regarding the subset of personal services can only be envisaged if they were to be supplied at markedly lowered wage rates. In any case, additional employment in public sector personal (as well as production-related) services is to be excluded as a realistic possibility under conditions where calls for budget cuts responding to fiscal crises, the streamlining of public administration, and the privatisation of public sector service organisations all dominate the scene.

Next come economic explanations. Unemployment (and more generally, pre-cariousness of situation) exists when more people are looking for jobs than can find them.

This imbalance can be interpreted in two ways: either the demand for workers is too low or the supply is too large. Most economic and social policy experts intuitively and almost automatically favour the first interpretation. The conclusion usually drawn in our "post-Keynesian" era, in which national demand-side programmes of full employment policies are largely understood to do more harm than good, is that the cost of labour (that is, wages plus employers' social security contributions plus non-monetary benefits and provisions) must be reduced or the incentives increased for employers to create and fill (domestic) jobs – whatever the effect on workers' incomes.

As regards reducing the total cost of employment, the prevailing supply-oriented theories proceed from the standard assumption that "cheaper" labour automatically yields more jobs. It is argued that the cost of employment must approach an "equilibrium wage", defined as one that actually absorbs the labour supply and thus clears the labour market. What adherents of this line of thought fail to take into account, however, is the fact that in every advanced economy there are actually two equilibrium wages, which lie far apart. The equilibrium wage that clears the labour market differs significantly from that which would also clear the markets for goods and services; and if the latter are not cleared, the labour market cannot be, either. For if the goods produced cannot be marketed, that will also lead to an insufficient demand for labour. Furthermore, a "perverse" supply reaction is known to be common in labour markets. As wages decrease, labour supply – be it in terms of the number of people seeking employment or the number of hours for which they seek employment – does not (due to the so-called "added worker effect") go down, but up (at least until "discouraged worker effects"[3] set in), contrary to what we see happening in markets for, say, bananas. After all, through expanding their labour supply, households strive to achieve or maintain what they consider their "adequate" consumption level. As a consequence, not a fixed but a growing labour supply would have to be absorbed through lowering the costs of employment. All of this is simply to point to the dual nature of wages. Wages represent not just a production cost to the employer, but also income for consumption in the employees' households. When economists focus narrowly on one or the other of these two functions of wages, they end up in the rather uninspiring controversy that pits the "right-wing liberal" supply-oriented theorists, who call for reducing the cost of employing labour, against the "left-wing Keynesian" demand-oriented recipes, which defend or call for an increase in real wage income – both in the name of achieving or restoring "full employment".

To be sure, since the end of the 1970s, supply-side economic doctrines have prevailed everywhere in Western Europe, the United States and Japan. Keynesian policy prescriptions, most clearly those emphasizing job creation and redistribution, have lost virtually all of their former intellectual and practical respectability. Five reasons for this are well known. First of all, globalisation of economic relations and the system of floating exchange rates have rendered futile any attempt to maintain control over the national economy by the Keynesian demand management instruments. Moreover, such demand management by its very nature proves effective only when it is implemented "unexpectedly". In contrast, when it becomes routine government practice that can be anticipated by rational agents, it merely yields subsidies for investors, but not a rise in employment. Furthermore, inflation, increased national debt, and the "crowding out" of private sector investment as a consequence of this debt are also considered to have led to the political as well as intellectual defeat of Keynesianism.

"Globalisation" is a concept used (on an inflationary scale) to make sense of the present situation; however, that overly general term in fact encompasses at least three distinct phenomena that need to be considered individually. First, the economic integration of Western Europe brings not only intensified competition to commodity and labour markets, but also a loss of national sovereignty in the realm of economic and social policy. This loss tends to provide policy-makers with a fairly watertight excuse for inaction as far as full employment policies are concerned. The question "What should be done?" becomes to a large extent irrelevant, simply because not one of the individual nations could go it alone and a "pacted" transnational employment policy has so far failed to bear fruit. It remains to be seen whether transnationally integrated European institutions and policies can do what the member countries of the European Union (EU) can no longer do on their own. As far as policies to combat unemployment are concerned, it is hard to detect promising signs of the determination to adopt and implement them, to say nothing of the viability of such policies. As far as the politics of economic policy are concerned, this is unsurprising, at least within the EU. Given EU governments' commitment to EMU and the Maastricht criteria that regulate access to it, there are simply no priorities conceivable for further burdening state budgets with initiatives for expanding employment, least of all in the public sector. And given the end of state socialism in Central and Eastern Europe and the total loss of its appeal in the eyes of former Western adherents, governments are no longer challenged to rival the only "accomplishment" of state socialism, namely stable full employment, in order to immunise the working class from its suspected inclination to "switch sides". At any rate, there is far less of a political imperative in the West than was the case during the cold war to maintain, through full employment, generous social benefits and a policy of redistribution, harmonious industrial relations and political stability, and thus hinder the "other side" and its communist leaders' ideological blandishments.

Second, the productivity of the East Asian economies is not only steadily destroying the competitive advantage West European economies once derived from their infrastructure and technology; it is also making certain competitive disadvantages of location, at least in Germany, all the more obvious.

And third, since the end of the cold war, not only the iron curtain countries but also the Western European capitalist countries have become "post-communist"; the latter must adjust to the immediate proximity of economic systems in which the training of the workforce may approach or even surpass levels to which they are accustomed, but where the cost of labour, at least for the present, amounts to only about one-seventh (as in the Czech Republic). This list of phenomena could be extended to include the special German problem of largely consumption-related West-East transfers, as well as the thorny fact that today many industrial regions with strong defence-related industries are being affected by an unequivocally negative "peace dividend".

Altogether, this post-communist globalisation results in persistently high levels of unemployment within the European Union. Successful employment policies in individual countries or regions are achieved only at the cost of mounting unemployment in other countries.

It is hard to see how the effects of "globalisation" (in any of its three versions with their highly differing impacts) could be responded to through reasonably promising policies. No argument or policy proposal, whether stemming from national interest or global justice, is likely to prevent either the NICs or the EU countries from supplying OECD markets with industrial products (including those of a technologically advanced sort) at (eventually) highly competitive prices. (This could even hold partly welcome implications for the exporters of investment goods from OECD countries.) Economic policy-makers have learned that protectionism can and will be punished by global markets. There is also no plausible moral rationale why the old industrial countries should be allowed to pull the ladder up behind them by obstructing, through protectionist measures, the industrialising efforts of South and East Asian, Latin American, and EU newcomers to the industrial world. It is a different matter whether such competitive advantages should be allowed to emerge from the blatant violation of workers' rights, environmental standards, or human rights (e.g. regarding child labour). At the same time, Western policy-makers can recognise from their own experience that compliance with such standards of rights and concerns has been the fruit of successful industrialisation, and hence should be allowed (and can be expected under the impact of appropriate political incentives) to follow the same path elsewhere.

As far as the politics of economic policy are concerned, it must also be pointed out that while "all of us" are in some way negatively affected by the two forms of labour market precariousness, "none of us" (or the major collective actors representing us) has for institutional reasons an obvious priority interest in restoring full employment (and in incurring the costs involved). As efficiency wage theorists have pointed out, employers, only seemingly counter-intuitively, have a rational interest in fixing wages at levels exceeding the market-clearing "equilibrium wage", as such "excessive" wage rates are supposed to economise on the transaction costs involved in high levels of labour force fluctuation. Trade unions must be concerned with defending wages and according priority to this objective, for the sake of their organisational robustness, over the objective of full employment. As far as the unemployed, underemployed, and those employed in the unprotected sector are concerned, it is well known that they suffer from severe handicaps in their access to forms of collective action and hence the resources, political as well as economic, that organised collective action can make available. Here, it is worth noting an institutional deficiency of labour markets. Three employee interests are involved: wages, working conditions, and level and security of employment. Only the first two, however, can be brought to the negotiating table; employers' interest associations cannot possibly agree (without running the risk of mass defection of its members) to making binding and enforceable collective agreements on a sectoral or district level concerning the number of workers who are to be employed for, say, the coming year.[4]

A final family of causal interpretations, in addition to technological, economic, political, and institutional ones, must be mentioned. This has to do with the cultural and moral prerequisites of the labour market as a key component of social order. Bluntly stated, the argument is that precariousness (in either of its two forms) results from degradation of the motivational and cognitive infrastructure of workers in Western societies, a moral disease sometimes suspected to result from the demoralising impact of overly generous arrangements of the welfare state itself. The decline of "the" work ethic is pinpointed as a key problem, as workers are said to demand "too much" (in terms of income, security and free time) while contributing "too little" themselves (in terms of work effort, endurance, the acquisition of cognitive skills and training, loyal and law-abiding behaviour, and adjustments imposed by flexibility requirements).

However, neither the truth content nor the policy implications of this set of arguments are evident. True, industrial capitalism breeds – and to an extent thrives upon – hedonistic consumerism and widespread betrayal of the alleged virtues of the Victorian working man. But also, arguably, the deficiencies of human capital acquisition may be due to inadequacies of the provision of schooling and training facilities, as well as the increasing cognitive demands of many jobs with which not everyone can be expected to cope successfully. The problem with many standard forms of public and private continuing training and skill-upgrading is that they often reach those already trained while bypassing those most in need of an upgrading. What should also not be underestimated is the extent of discouragement, disorientation, frustration and cynicism that is being caused by – rather than causing – the anticipation of either form of precariousness, and which very understandably might contribute to the symptoms of an alleged motivational decay. Moreover, the policy implications of this kind of diagnosis are far from obvious, other than the abolition of institutional devices of welfare and social protection, and the upgrading of skills and cognitive capabilities through human capital investments.

Another social and cultural explanation of labour market precariousness concerns the decline of a life form that must be considered, apart from the labour contract, another major mechanism through which people are situated or inserted into social life: the nuclear family. This implies an overall increase, although one sharply varying across countries, of female labour market participation and its duration over women's life course. In many European countries, on average, people marry later or (increasingly) not at all, they have fewer children, and marriages last shorter periods. Thus, a growing supply of female labour power that used to be tied to the family household and absorbed by non-market work now appears on the supply side of the labour market. The weakening of the family household and of the pattern of social support it is capable of providing may be read not so much as a symptom of "individualisation" but as both the cause of additional (female) labour supply and a response to the perceived precariousness of employment, income, and protection. Moreover, gender equality and equal access of women to both higher education and the job market has become, partly as a consequence of feminist cultural and political mobilisation, a moral and political tenet (though certainly not a socio-economic reality) advocated by most major political forces except for the far right. It follows that discriminatory policies designed to ban parts of the female labour supply from the market must be considered morally and politically obsolete, particularly as precariousness of situation and subsistence makes an increasing number of households dependent upon supplying the market with more than one "unit" of labour power.

To summarise, one can think of a limited universe of conceivable strategies towards "full" (or, at any rate, "more") employment, most of which appear to be positively foreclosed under prevailing and foreseeable conditions. First, a growth policy operating on the demand side of the labour market is virtually impossible to implement in open economies exposed to globalisation; even if it were possible to implement, its yields in terms of employment remain very uncertain, and at any rate limited. Second, one could operate, as neo-liberals propose to do, on the supply side of labour. This means increasing the attractiveness of labour to employers by improving those characteristics of the workforce which employers value most. The most preferred workers are cheap (in terms of wages and social security contributions), skilled (both in terms of technical competence and desirable work attitudes) and flexible (*i.e.* subjectively willing to adjust to changes in wages, skill requirements, work time and location of job, as well as objectively free from overly "rigid" types of protection and regulation governing the contractual employment relationship). Pursuit of this strategy, however, is likely to lead to both serious political constraints and highly negative consequences for social cohesion; the phenomena of the "new underclass" and "working poor" are the most obvious indicators of the latter. Third, there are negative supply-side policies which try to limit access to the labour market. The more traditional variants of this option include keeping women in the family household, sending foreigners home, extending the period of training for young workers and promoting early retirement for elderly ones. The first two of these meet with powerful political and moral objections as well as a variety of institutional obstacles, and the latter two with equally prohibitive economic ones, namely educational and pension expenditures. Work time reduction is a less constrained strategic option for cutting supply, but it also meets with fairly insurmountable obstacles which are explained below. All of these considerations lead to the conclusion (in Section 3) that a new generation of negative supply-side strategies is necessary, desirable, and feasible – strategies designed to create a sufficiently attractive economic citizens' right to opt out of formal employment for limited periods of time.

2. SOCIO-POLITICAL CONSEQUENCES OF PRECARIOUSNESS

As regards the impact of unemployment upon individuals failing to obtain – and keep – stable jobs, much depends upon the duration of unemployment and the amount and duration of transfer income and training services to which they are entitled. A special case, mostly unaccounted for by labour market statistics, is youth unemployment, or the condition of being out of a job without ever having had one that was regular and protected. The consequences of the experience of being in a precarious position are well known, and need not be dwelled upon here. They include the absence of the autonomy contingent upon "normal" participation in work and consumption. Thus social isolation, loss of social esteem as well as self-esteem, self-blame, the gradual erosion of a disciplined and organised way of life, a negative impact upon physical and mental health, and the gradual loss of employability are all well-documented consequences of precariousness. "Unemployability" results from the fact that (skilled) labour power is itself a "perishable good" that can vanish due to non-utilisation, and from the fact that a substantial spell of unemployment in a person's career is often used to stigmatise him or her according to some "last in first out" rule of hiring and firing. Illegal forms of employment, as well as criminal forms of acquisition of income (including income from drug markets) are also known to be statistical implications of joblessness.

On a more systemic level, the consequences of unemployment and income precariousness for the systems of social security and welfare are also well known, at least on the European continent. Whether or not the finances of social security – in its old age, health, unemployment, and in some countries long-term care branches – are as strongly contributory (as opposed to tax-financed) as they are in Germany, the failure of the labour market to "situate" people or to provide for their income and protection places a growing fiscal strain upon social security systems. The nightmarish scenario that haunts policy-makers is that of a vicious circle: in order to honour legal claims of the unemployed and the recipients of social assistance, contributions (as well as taxes) must be raised to (or kept at) levels that in turn increase the costs of employment (as opposed to direct wage costs) to levels at which the continued employment of segments of the workforce becomes uncompetitive and unaffordable. Thus unemployment generates further unemployment, given the constraints of an already highly unfavourable demographic age structure and the limited political leeway for sharp and sudden reductions of the legal entitlements of those affected by precariousness of employment and income.

These limitations, however, do not preclude the downscaling and partial reconstruction (*Umbau*) of the entire welfare state structure, which is well under way in most EU as well as other OECD countries, from the United States to New Zealand. The various types of welfare systems that are present in these countries were historically built out of four successive major components, the sequence of which reaches back to the beginnings of industrialisation (as well as the progressive "marketisation" of labour) in the nineteenth century. The driving forces behind this sequence were politicised class conflict (sometimes perceived by governing elites as well as by its protagonists as potentially "revolutionary") and international conflict within the modern state system which together have triggered welfare state developments – with war and postwar situations as typical quantum leaps of institutional innovation.

First, workers were protected through statutory regulations concerning work time and other conditions. Second, protection extended outside of work through statutory arrangements absorbing (some of) the income-related risk of illness, industrial accidents, lack of income in old age, and (usually much later) unemployment; these social policies also include the granting of entitlements to housing and family allowances. Third, workers won the guaranteed right to have wages determined not through individual contract alone but through collective wage bargaining, and were legally granted supply-side cartelisation of the labour market through trade unions and the right to strike. Finally, a *de facto* (and in some countries *de jure*) commitment of governments was institutionalised to pursue the "full employment" objective with the highest priority through the economic policies of the nation state. It is now evident that, as the devices of this last and most recent component of the welfare state structure are manifestly failing, the three earlier sets of welfare state accomplishments – workers' protection, social security and collective wage bargaining based on industrial unionism – are also being adversely affected.

Unemployment means more than people being out of work and in need of support while out of work. It implies the erosion of the institutional shell in which the labour market has been embedded and that has come to be taken for granted as the underpinning of the order and stability of the industrial type of society: the welfare state.

It is presently not clear what, if any, the large-scale or long-term consequences of the erosion of this protective shell might be – its consequences for political legitimacy, social order, or the type and intensity of social conflict. One thing seems safe to exclude: organised mass movements overthrowing in revolutionary ways the foundations of industrial capitalism cum liberal democracy and aiming at replacing them with an alternative institutional design for the political economy. As far as political consequences can at all be observed and predicted, there could be scattered and militant – though strategically aimless and short-lived – movements protesting mass dismissals and cuts in social spending. To speculate for a moment, a long-term shift of the scene, or institutional location, of social conflict appears to be a likely course of development. Schematically speaking, the conflict over life chances could "move up" from the specialised negotiating tables of robust social partners to national governments and further on to transnational agencies of governance; at the same time, the scenery of conflict could also "move down" to the streets, and eventually to the state's organs of repression and criminal justice.

What also seems to be on the rise is the politics of rightist populist protectionism calling for borders to be strengthened against the outward flow of capital and, in particular and with xenophobic overtones, the inward flow of employment-seeking "foreign" labour.

More significant than strategic mass action challenging the political order are collectively relevant consequences of a non-political or, at best, pre-political sort. Fear, fatalism, submissiveness, and an inclination to blame victims are familiar psychological responses to the experience of precariousness, which produce less-well-understood repercussions upon political behaviour and political culture. Further effects relate to the tearing up of social cohesion – of the sense shared by those affected by precariousness as well as by those not (yet) affected that they live in one and the same society, subject to the same rights and duties, opportunities and constraints. This disintegration can take place according to markers of space (as with urban or regional segregation), of time (between cohorts and generations), of educational attainment, health, and family resources, of legality (having vs. not having a legal residence and criminal record), of industrial and occupational sector, or of race or ethnicity. With the sharpening divisions of life chances and symptoms of marginalisation becoming evident to both winners and losers in the game of avoiding and escaping precariousness, the moral resources of solidarity – the taste for things such as the well-being of "everyone else" and the "pleasure of living in a just society" – are bound to decline. There is growing evidence that targeted austerity measures and welfare cuts meet not with consistent resistance, but with more or less tacit approval from the majority, who have reason to expect more good than harm from tightening other people's belts; what conflict there is concerns whose belts, not the tightening as such.

3. THE KEY POLICY CHOICE

The causes of precariousness summarised in Section 1, seen in light of the three kinds of consequences (assumed to be morally as well as functionally unacceptable) outlined in Section 2, leave policy-makers and political forces in general with the following basic choice. They can act upon the belief that those consequences of social disorganisation can be controlled and eventually eliminated by restoring and reinvigorating the labour market as the core generator of social order.[5] Or, alternatively, they can act upon the belief that such restoration efforts are hopeless or intrinsically unacceptable because of their economic and moral implications. In the latter case, the answer must be sought not in the elimination of the causes themselves – for they cannot be removed – but in the gradual neutralisation of the impact they have upon individual life chances, institutional order and social cohesion. The choice is between restoring "full" employment and making non-employment tolerable by controlling its consequences in terms of precariousness.

This paper argues for the second of these two basic alternatives. For the sake of realism and honesty, unemployment and the two forms of precariousness should no longer be described as a "problem" (implying that it can be solved through the right amount of policy inventiveness, effort and determination) but as a grim phenomenon and challenge confronting the economies, polities and societies of the OECD world. It does no good to address this painful and chronic condition with the full-employment rhetoric cherished by Social Democrats as well as free market economists in most of the OECD countries. We will simply have to get used to (and effectively cope with) the fact that a large part of our adult population of both sexes will not find a berth and bread in "normal", *i.e.* reasonably secure, adequately protected, and acceptably paid jobs. The key question remains whether and how we can structure this situation so as to minimise its negative social and political impact by combining the contractual and market patterns governing the social situation and status of labour with institutional patterns based on the principles of citizenship and community.

Europe's predominant reaction to this situation is a clear case of the first alternative answer. Generally speaking, there are three dimensions which can be manipulated in order to make employing labour marginally more attractive to employers: wages, skills, and time. In political terms, the first of these boils down to policies of more or less controlled reduction of real wages, the costs of employment, social security, and other transfers and services. Under the competitive pressure from the world market, some EU countries are moving away from allegedly de luxe working conditions and uniformly high income levels. What has been termed the high-wage, high-skill, high-protection package of the "standard employment relation" ("*Normalarbeitsverhältnis*") has lost its empirical as well as moral "normalcy". These changes are supported politically by a growing "popular front of capital" with its call for increasing employment through cutting wages and other employment costs. Along these lines, Fritz Scharpf, a prominent Social Democratic political theorist, made a courageous suggestion: combine the ideas of "negative income tax" and welfare state solidarity to create a low-wage sector in the German economy, with wages degressively subsidised from tax revenues. Yet there is no indication whether employers would even be interested in creating such low-cost jobs, or, if they were, whether they could be counted on to fill these jobs chiefly with additional workers (rather than by downgrading those already employed), and with workers from the domestic labour market (rather than those coming from other EU countries or with *extracommunitari*).[6] Only if employers can be coaxed over these three hurdles by the lure of wage subsidies will the promised positive effects on (domestic) unemployment be achieved.

Skills are the second dimension. An alternative to making employment "cheaper" at constant levels of productivity is making workers better skilled and more productive at (presumably) constant wage costs. This is the policy approach of what is sometimes called "human capitalism", with associated overtones of "humane capitalism" (Waters).

Doubtlessly, this approach has its attractions, as well as shortcomings. First, higher skills require extended periods of training, and for these periods labour power is withdrawn from the supply side of the labour market. But the temporarily "deactivated" labour power must be supported during these periods, and his or her training activities paid for, and it is not clear where the resources should come from that are needed to fund any large scale "qualification offensive". This is a particularly thorny problem because it is in the nature of human (in contrast to physical) capital that the investor creating such capital does not acquire property rights; the property of one's own skills remains, according to the liberal principle of "self-ownership", that of the person to whom the skills are attached. The bottom line is a classic collective action problem: each prospective employer of skilled labour power will rationally seek to take a free ride on other employers' training efforts. The result is a systematic underinvestment in human skills. But secondly, it is by no means clear that skills acquired through years of formal training are actually and across the board a bottleneck variable. Many jobs do not require or make effective use of the skills that jobholders do actually possess. Or, a mismatch of skills and job requirements occurs due to the unpredictability of changes in the latter. Training is, after all, a "fuzzy technology"; algorithms that tie efforts to outcomes, or outcomes to economic use, are notoriously hard to calculate. Thirdly, it must be noted that the ability and willingness of people to undergo and endure cycles of obsolescence of their skills, upgrading and "catching up", and possibly renewed obsolescence must be limited. "Qualification offensives" produce as many losers (or "failures") as they produce winners, and they generally benefit most those who need them least (for the sake of maintaining employment), and vice versa. The third of the above dimensions, time, cannot be discussed in detail here. The basic idea is that employers will be interested in employing more workers (or in maintaining present levels of employment) if workers are willing to adjust to the rhythm of production, and agree to variations in their work time. The option of putting workers to work whenever it is necessary, and for the duration of time necessary, may well make the individual employee marginally more valuable; but it is also a powerful device for economising on the total workforce needed by an enterprise.

Current initiatives and proposals on labour market and wage policies have one thing in common: their thrust is defensive. At best they preserve existing jobs, but they do not create any new ones. Perhaps they encourage employers to hire workers or not to lay off employees; but when reductions in real wages result, it becomes more difficult for the producers of consumer goods to sell their output. Even in the absence of such disappointing economic consequences, a question remains. Were the extensive employment and social protections that the labour force enjoys in most EU countries to be dismantled in a regulated manner, could such a policy hold at bay such desperate (and already manifest) reactions as a left-wing militant struggle for government protection of jobs at virtually any price, or a right-wing chauvinistic struggle for government protection against foreign workers seeking employment? If such struggles became a mass phenomenon, in either version, societies would presumably be facing challenges on a scale almost unknown in Europe since the Second World War. More would be at stake than what is considered an equitable distribution of social wealth; the very survival of democratic institutions and political processes would be jeopardised.

Such are the grim perspectives that present themselves when one clings to the notion that a steady volume of wage earners must be squeezed into lower-paying jobs, better skills, or less rigid temporal patterns of labour force utilisation. A different, much less common reading of the imbalance in the labour market is as follows.

What is needed is not an increase in the number of jobs but a reduction in the volume of work (*i.e.* the product of employment-seeking persons and the number of work hours or years per person). This perspective leads to a "negative" supply-side labour market policy, favoured not so much by employers but by unions and policy-makers. The most drastic mechanism with which one could achieve such supply-side relief is an outright selective ban. First comes actual prohibition of workers entering the labour market, specifically foreigners and (married) women, perhaps also the elderly; for legal and moral reasons this measure cannot be implemented. Any possibility of influencing the labour supply through control of the number of people being admitted to the labour market must be dismissed, with the limited exception of restrictive immigration policies aimed at employment-seeking *extracommunitari*. What remains is control of working time: the supply can be rationed per day, per week, per year, per life in such a way that – all other conditions remaining constant – any surplus supply of labour could be reduced or perhaps avoided altogether in the future. In the mid-1980s, this conceptual model dominated the German trade unions' policy of work time reduction. The weakness of the logic of spreading employment opportunities by shortening work time is that in practice the model becomes morally excessively demanding for the individual employee: work time reduction, and especially the promotion of part-time work, is an indirect method of income rationing. After all, why should "I" agree to work shorter hours (and thereby give up income or potential pay raises) just so that "you" can also work and earn income, especially since it is uncertain whether "he", the employer, will (or can) reward my sacrifice by granting you the benefit of additional employment? Will he really use my and others' reduced working time in order to create a larger (or even just a stable) workforce? Or will "he" be able to compensate for shrinking hours through labour-saving investment and greater time flexibility of the labour process? If so, we all might end up worse off than before.

The game thus involves a classical collective goods problem, where the pessimists defect and their defection spreads more pessimism, which soon grows beyond the capacity of trade unions for control and mobilisation. The result is that on the supply side of the labour market little can be accomplished, either with respect to personnel or as regards working time.[7] That will remain true as long as the view (inculcated by all the major institutions) persists that the value and success of an individual's life is expressed on the labour market and in terms of his or her success as a wage earner. This concept of normality is as wrongheaded as it is compelling. It is wrongheaded because it drives many people into a race which they can only lose. It is compelling, on the other hand, because in our work-centred society the dominant institutions in fact reserve the things that make life worth living (freedom, independence, security, recognition, self-esteem) for those people who prove themselves in economic life as holders of jobs and earners of income. Those who fail (by being unemployed) to fulfil or decide not to adhere to the norm (for instance mothers, or "mere housewives", to say nothing of "house-husbands") need pretty robust excuses if they want to avoid appearing to be losers, to themselves as well as to others. Anyone who does not work at least intermittently or part-time incurs considerable disadvantages as far as income and social security are concerned – and often, moral (self-)blame as well.

The moral, cultural and institutional foundations of the work-centred society reward the wage earner, but many citizens no longer have access to these rewards. Society mobilises a constant surplus of labour that it cannot absorb, *i.e.* that it cannot use for the production of goods and services. The notion that one can share in the commodities and values of life only if one has successfully marketed one's own labour has become morally indefensible. What justifies the idea that the sum total of useful activities a human being can perform must pass through the needle's eye of an employment contract? It is not difficult to point at useful activities (such as donating blood[8]) for which the quality of outcome is linked to the fact that they are not performed as paid work. This may apply, for instance, to all forms of caring. Is it fair to limit opportunities for consumption, social security, and social standing to those who have already won them on the labour market?

One argument for full employment, gaining increasing if sometimes openly cynical support, suggests that the integration of the largest possible number of people into the labour market is desirable, not for reasons of economic production and social justice, but for reasons of social control. The pessimistic view of human nature that underlies this argument is plain: if human beings do not work under supervision and within the framework of formal contractual obligations, they will necessarily fall into a sterile or chaotic way of life. To be sure, this argument in retrospect discredits the humane value of earlier technical and economic progress that liberated people from back-breaking work. At the same time it tacitly recognises the wretchedness of a social order that cannot keep its citizens in line except through the disciplinary powers exercised by labour organisations.

In this situation, praise of the modesty and benefits of living outside employed work on limited means does not help either. Assuring people that it can be very satisfying to "do something meaningful for others" in the family or in volunteer work, or to enjoy a contemplative existence, will hardly persuade them to stay home. Opportunity structures are not there to back such moralising rhetoric, let alone any outright attempt to tighten other people's belts. On the contrary, the citizens of our work-centred society find the material and immaterial rewards attached to the allegedly "normal" existence of the wage earner too attractive for significant numbers of them to consider giving up – or giving up the quest for – full-time work and the corresponding income. Indeed, as the likelihood decreases that every adult will be able to find and keep a secure, satisfying, and well-paying job, the competition – between generations, sexes, ethnic groups – will become more intense and aggressive. Some conservative prophets, noting the overwhelmingly high value placed on formal work, believe that life outside the labour market (in the family, in the community, in one's own garden, in co-operatives, networks, and associations) has to be accorded a value greater than is possible through moralistic praise for self-sacrifice, modest expectations, and appeals to a sense of community. The revaluation of leisure time and the individually selected activity with which it might be filled – or, conversely, the societal devaluation of participation in the labour market – is a project that goes to the moral, institutional and economic heart of democratic industrial societies. These societies have no institutional models to rely on when confronting the problem of wealth being produced by a declining percentage of their citizens while all citizens claim a sufficient share of this wealth.

One need not be a prophet to recognise the central problem with which the institutions of our political economies will be preoccupied for the foreseeable future, nationally and globally. The portion of the population that is actually involved in the creation of economic value will continue to shrink; at the same time, the "capillary" mechanisms of distribution – the family, the welfare state, even development aid policies that once provided subsistence and opportunities for participation in society to persons and regions outside the "productive core" of the global economy – are being crippled. The question that remains is how – using what institutional logic or moral justification – can resources and opportunities be channelled, reliably and fairly, from the productive core to the "unproductive" periphery.

4. ECONOMIC CITIZENSHIP RIGHTS BEYOND FULL EMPLOYMENT

This chapter now explores the alternative policy choice mentioned above: rather than eliminate the causes of deficient levels of market absorption of labour, neutralise the consequences. The corresponding approach to the problems of precariousness calls on strategies advocating a basic income as an economic citizenship (as opposed to employee) right. Basic income models differ in one important respect from all suggestions for negative taxation in the low-income sector, which amount to a reduction in wages without a corresponding reduction in income. In the former, income transfer is tied not to individual employment-related circumstances (need, current employment, willingness and ability to work, and so on), but exclusively to the individual's citizenship status. This arrangement would have the advantage that income support is no longer subject to fluctuations in the demand for (cheap) labour; instead, income transfer goes into effect – and with it, a reduction in manifest unemployment – as soon as citizens choose to take advantage of it. They can decide, according to their personal and labour market circumstances, whether they want to supplement their subsistence income by taking on a regular job. Structuring income transfer in such a fashion would make allowances for the fact that, because of lack of suitability and lack of demand, many workers can never be permanently integrated into the labour market, even at extremely low wages. It makes no sense to pretend otherwise, thereby subjecting them to a lasting, humiliating experience of failure.

Normative justifications for this proposal can easily be invoked. First, OECD societies are "rich" societies that can afford the costs of citizenship-based remedies to (income) precariousness. These societies have remained wealthy – that is the difference between the present situation and the worldwide Depression at the end of the 1920s. But they lack an institutional mechanism that would allow them to distribute their wealth to all their citizens. Second, distributive status can no longer be tied to the labour contract without the implication of unfair exclusion. As long as most workers do actually have a chance to contribute to the production of society's wealth through paid employment, the problem of distributing wealth is solved by each individual's labour contract and the family support and social security arrangements tied to it. Once this ceases to be the case, and there is no longer even the possibility of the supposedly "normal" condition of full-time and lifelong "full" employment, plus family support for those outside the labour market, plus sufficient access to social security and unemployment benefits for all those who are neither employed nor "dependents", the problem of distribution can be solved only by establishing specific economic rights that all citizens grant each other as a component of their citizenship. The central idea of a "citizens' income" consists in the right to sufficient income not conditional upon gainful employment (former employment, availability to work, or proof of circumstances, such as presence in the household of small children, that would justify exemption from the rule of gainful employment). Concretely, this would mean that suggestions such as "negative income tax", "citizens' income"[9] or "degressive income subsidies" surfacing from many corners within the social policy reform debate today would not hinge on a person becoming a "worker" (or preparing to do so, e.g. students or persons in vocational training), but would take effect as an automatic consequence of citizenship.

Anyone prepared to approach a concept so entirely foreign to the traditions and institutions of our industrial society and its work ethic must consider three counter-arguments. The first objection refers to incentive effects: why should rational actors still want to work if they can secure a bare living without formal employment? One may answer with the assumption that a temporary withdrawal from wage labour would indeed – in view of the situation described above – be desirable (since there are no real alternatives anyway).[10] On the other hand, the withdrawal would be limited, since the added incentive of a higher income will not fail to have its mobilising effect upon labour market participation.

The second objection must be taken more seriously, and is financial in nature. If a minority receives a non-employment-related citizens' income, then the (positive) tax-paying structural majority will be inclined to favour policy measures that would lower this citizen's income to a level so low as to necessitate the search for gainful employment – which is what the market-liberal proponents of the negative income tax had in mind in the first place. However, there are easily conceivable remedies that would protect against these eventualities, e.g. an indexing of citizens' income levels which could only be infringed with difficulty through legislation due to a requirement of super-majorities for cuts in benefits. Alternatively or additionally, the basic income could be designed in such a way that every citizen, regardless of the amount of their income, receives it, while only those who have opted out of gainful employment are entitled to the net benefit and everyone else will undergo taxation at correspondingly increased rates.

Finally, there is the most important objection: a "banning" of a portion of the adult population from the labour market, even with comfortable material protection, might be seen as amounting to moral cynicism, as such a policy aims at "putting out of operation" the human capacity of doing useful things, or scrapping it altogether. By overcoming precariousness of distributional status, the scheme

would cement a precariousness of situation in production that amounts to permanent exclusion. Such an approach would run contrary to principles of material
equality (in particular to those prohibiting gender discrimination) as well as to an
individual's moral right to develop him- or herself through activities which are
recognised as useful.

The helplessness implicit in this argument can be lessened somewhat by
measures which make entitlement to citizens' income dependent on a minimum
age of the recipient (say, 25) and which encourage and promote "rotation" between
gainful employment and other activities outside the labour market.

To be sure, this new approach to the solution of the distribution problem and
the uncoupling of claims to income from the performance of marketable labour is
not likely to be accepted and implemented any time soon. Strongly rooted intu-
itions about economic justice and the rights and duties of individuals stand in its
way. Moreover, it is hard to assess the overall long-term and second-order economic and behavioural consequences which can only be revealed through carefully
monitored practical policy experimentation. For both of these reasons, a gradualist
and reversible approach is called for. Such an approach can proceed in either of two
directions: *a)* recognised conditional exemption from labour market participation
(or the freedom to "opt out") or *b)* temporal exemption. The first approach would
substantially expand the list of "excuses" for non-participation that already exist in
any modern society. As it is, these excuses, apart from those of disability and old
age, relate to being sick, giving birth and being a parent of an infant, doing military
service, and undergoing training. All these conditions are associated with claims to
income without performing market-valued productive services, though such income
is usually limited as to its level and duration, and contingent upon further conditions. New additions to the list would include activities in the voluntary sector and
personal care, but also associational activities pertaining to sports, culture, education and environmental protection. Moreover, entitlements would be "de-
conditioned", since they are presently tied to duration of claims and precede gainful
employment. The problem with this approach is that well-founded doubts, suspi-
cions and controversies are likely to arise as to whether "worthy non-market"
activities are in fact to be considered "useful", as well as whether they are actually
being performed.

The other approach, equally gradualist and experimental, would rely on the
time dimension, which provides for interesting possibilities of incentive-steering
and fine-tuning. The basic idea is that every citizen is born with an entitlement to a
"sabbatical account" as a right of citizenship. This account covers, say, ten years of
subsistence-level income (to be fixed at a level somewhat higher than welfare or
social assistance payments that would still be needed) and can be drawn upon at
any time after the age of early adulthood (say, 18) and before retirement age. In
order to avoid any incentive to forgo vocational training or equivalent qualifica-

tions, access to the account is limited to those with a vocational training certificate or at least three years of employment experience. In order to build in some degree of control over the temporal pattern according to which individuals spend their "time capital", a discounting and interest mechanism could be envisaged. As it appears less desirable that individuals spend their sabbatical years very early in their life course, a strong discount rate would have to be introduced, such that every one year withdrawn from the sabbatical account under the age of 30 diminishes the remaining stock by two full years. Also, the "time taxation" could be made progressive, which would mean that the more years a person takes off the account, the steeper the extra deduction. Inversely, every year spent after the age of, say, 45 would "cost" just 0.6 years. Special discounts and interest rates could be introduced for childbearing and personal care activities, as well as for training and the upgrading of personal skills. There would also have to be a premium on not withdrawing, or not fully withdrawing one's account, in the form of incremental additions to old age pensions.

Financially, the costs of the personal sabbatical account could partly be covered by funds that are so far earmarked for social assistance, family and training allowances and early retirement schemes, and perhaps even for long-term unemployment and sick pay. The considerable advantage of the sabbatical account over the first approach (*i.e.* an expanded list of "excuses") must be seen in the fact that full liberty is granted to the choice of individual priorities of time use as they emerge over the life course, and that such freedom of choice will at the same time be exercised in – and disciplined by – the awareness that the "time funds" made available to individuals as an economic citizen right are strictly limited.

This at least can be expected to be the case if the amount of income the persons temporarily leaving the workforce are entitled to would clearly exceed "welfare" or social assistance levels; otherwise, the "liberty" of opting out would become nominal and restricted to just the lowest levels of income earners. That liberty could be further enhanced by a scheme of "preferential re-hiring" of those who, having opted out, wish to be re-employed.

A further advantage is that risks (unemployment, sickness, etc.) that are no longer schematically standardized are covered for categories of claimants; the needs, contingencies and priorities of individuals can be covered in individualised yet unbureaucratic ways. Finally, the "sabbatical account" would provide a real (if time-constrained) option to opt out from gainful employment, thus promoting rotation and avoiding, more reliably than an unconditional and temporally unlimited basic income could do, the division of the workforce into permanent labour market participants and permanent non-participants.

Whatever the approach and design, a solution to the problem of structural unemployment and underemployment, as well as that of the two kinds of precariousness associated with them, is called for – one that works on the supply side of the labour market, uncouples claims to income from remuneration for market labour (and even from willingness to participate in the labour market), and at the same time takes the three objections mentioned above seriously.

Taken together, this new yet gradualist solution to the dual problem of "situation" and "distribution" would amount to the long-term implementation of the following three principles.

First, no one has the right to exclude entire categories of the population (on such criteria as sex, age, nationality, skills and so on) from participation in the labour market. Trying to do so (or allowing precariousness in either of its forms to spread without anyone "doing" it) amounts to jeopardising minimum levels of social cohesion and civic integration, which are already severely at risk in many of the advanced societies.

Second, since adult citizens do not have a "right to work" but instead a right to compete for employment, all those who voluntarily withdraw from this competition are doing a favour to all those who wish to remain, and whose chances of being employed are correspondingly improved. Those who withdraw deserve compensation for the duration of their non-participation in the labour market. The central idea is a citizens' right to a basic income (however limited with regard to extra-market activity or its duration) that is untied to any further conditions (such as need, willingness to work, marital status), financed from general revenues, and sufficient to afford a modest living.

Third, compensation for the (always reversible) individual decision to withdraw from the labour market is not simply a "reward" to individuals for taking their labour out of the economy. It is meant to encourage them to put their labour to uses other than selling it in return for wages. The moral rule implied here is that people who claim income without gainful employment are also expected to perform useful activities, only without pay.

True, outside the immediate circle of the household and family, it is not easy to find ways to put one's labour to useful non-market activities. For as the industrial societies have developed, so has a trap for their workers. For a long time, the labour market has appeared so much more rewarding than any informal activities of self-provision – and as a result, the latter became virtually non-existent. Now that the market can no longer absorb the volume of available labour (or potential for performing useful activities), these non-market activities are not available on a sufficient scale as options for providing individuals with subsistence as well as social recognition. Nor is there is any reason to expect that informal alternative forms of useful activity will crop up spontaneously or be brought about by means of mere moral suasion extolling the merits of "self help", "community" and "voluntary" activities; such non-market activities must be institutionally "reinvented", sponsored, and encouraged.

To summarise, the institutional reordering of labour following such principles would of course not eliminate unemployment. It could, however, help transform the hardly avoidable long-term state of affairs, in which not all workers are able to secure regular and protected gainful employment, into a more tolerable, less conflict-ridden and less unfair situation.

5. ELEMENTS OF A SCENARIO

How "realistic" is the expectation that policy orientations of the kind explored in the previous section will become dominant? As a fundamental policy shift is obviously involved, chances are that the idea of bidding farewell to the labour contract as the cornerstone of social order will be rejected as plainly "utopian", and at least by some as a "black" utopia at that. This objection, however, is only as valid as the alternative can be considered "non-utopian" – the alternative, that is, of restoring acceptable levels of employment, income and security by more conventional means of economic and social policies. If the premises of the above analysis are right and these conventional policy approaches must eventually fail, the policy choice becomes one between two utopias, rather than between "realism" and "utopianism". The question then becomes: which of the two "utopias" is likely to prevail? To be sure, the perception of a crisis situation can make people, masses and elites alike, utterly conservative and entirely unwilling to learn and innovate. Out of fear of disorder and disorientation, societies adhere all the more passionately to familiar institutional patterns as they actually become less viable. Moreover, crises can have a profound disorganising effect upon the governing capacity of society. For instance, transnational and global market integration is sometimes seen to create a condition of "disembedded liberalism", the dynamics of which can no longer be controlled or regulated by any individual state. But if the subjective capacity to learn were always monotonously to decrease when the objective need for learning increases, basic societal innovations that have actually occurred in history could not be accounted for. It is therefore safe to assume that the two variables might be linked in a U-shaped pattern.

Assuming that the capacity for institutional innovation is not permanently and consistently disabled by the experience of crisis and malfunctioning, it is still necessary to identify the factors that are likely to determine the trajectory of learning, reorientation and innovation. These factors can plausibly be divided into three groups: widely shared normative traditions, current experience of facts and trends, and the activity of political elites who invoke these traditions and interpret current experience.

a) Normative traditions

These rely on the assumption that the modern societies belonging to the OECD world all partake in some version of universalist moral tradition. In Europe and North America at least, and perhaps in Japan as well (in a varying version), the duty to care for the rights and well-being of others is an inalienable part of the moral heritage. To put the same argument differently, privilege and inequality require justification in corresponding quantities – and the supply of such justifications is limited. To be sure, the range of those "others" that enjoy inclusion in a relevant universe may vary greatly – from family to nation to mankind. As a consequence of this normative legacy (stemming from the Judeo-Christian, Enlightenment-liberal, and socialist traditions), a concern with human and citizenship rights, as well as the material preconditions for the effective enjoyment of such rights, must be considered part of the repertoire of operative arguments that can be brought to bear upon the evaluation of policies and institutions. In spite of the prevailing neo-liberal economic doctrines and their obvious affinities with postmodernist cultural theories and practices, these legacies cannot intentionally be invalidated or "forgotten".

b) Experience

Over the past hundred and fifty years, a driving force behind social policy innovations has always been the perception or anticipation of imminent disintegration of social order and social cohesion. While the forms of such disintegration or breakup of social cohesion have certainly changed and neither organised class conflict nor postwar turbulences play a significant role today, other sorts of symptoms of disintegration dominate the scene and cannot fail to be perceived as a potentially threatening malaise. At any rate, the widespread presence of precariousness (in either of its two forms) is experienced as a source of negative externalities, affecting even those who are least affected by it directly.

Just a few illustrations must suffice here. What sociologists call "cultural reproduction" – the tradition of the cognitive culture and moral norms of a society – occurs in modern society largely as a by-product of formal education. Formal education in turn is functionally tied to (as well as individually motivated by) the anticipated insertion of "educated" labour power into occupational roles. If (less privileged) parts of the young generation have reason to anticipate, on the basis of current experience, that education is less and less likely to lead them anywhere in terms of employment, careers, and security, the motivational basis of effort and ambition is weakened, and "dropping out of school" becomes a mass phenomenon (an effect that is of course being exacerbated by cuts in the public funding of secondary and higher education). The spatial organisation of modern cities is often marked by patterns of segregation that separate those living under conditions of precariousness (applying even to citizenship and residence rights) from the "normal" participants in labour and goods markets as well as from the legal order. Resulting negative externalities include the familiar pathologies of a spatially concentrated "underclass", not least widespread violence and the drug economy.

Furthermore, people with a precarious status of labour market participation and social protection will have to depend upon unprotected, informal, and criminal methods of acquiring income. Of these, informal employment in "underground labour markets" (with low wages, no protection, and no taxes or social security contributions being paid) generate the most consequential negative externalities, as they outcompete sectors of formal employment and thus further undermine the fiscal basis of social security systems. Moreover, the experience and anticipation of precariousness is a powerful factor in the erosion of family life and reproduction, which in turn intensifies that precariousness when the family fails to function as a micro system of social security.

Finally, political externalities of persisting precariousness must be mentioned. These are not limited to the frustration and cynicism with which citizens and voters react to governing elites who so obviously fail to restore the presumably "normal" condition of a "fully employed" society. They also include the rise of ethnocentric and racist forms of (partly violent) "exclusivism" and the political mobilisation based on these motives that can be observed in many OECD countries. All of these collectively relevant externalities of precariousness are brought to the attention of mass audiences both through the results of social-scientific self-observation of modern societies and by extensive media reporting.

c) Scope for elite-initiated innovation

These symptoms of a pervasive crisis of institutional stability and social cohesion cannot fail – the longer they prevail, the more clearly they are perceived by mass audiences, and the more ineffectual conventional remedies turn out to be – to be perceived as a challenge by political and economic elites who begin to appreciate the trade-off between the costs of social disintegration and the efficiency gains brought about by a globalised economy that also generates precariousness on a vast scale. Evidence has accumulated indicating that social disintegration resulting from precariousness can neither be ignored (for both economic and political reasons) nor expected to be overcome as a by-product of political deregulation, economic globalisation or technological modernisation. That evidence will force elites to pay fresh attention to very basic questions of social order. Both in normative terms [i.e. concerning the legacies and arguments mentioned under a)] and in functional terms, the problem of how to cope with the economic efficiency vs. social cohesion trade-off will assert itself as the key problem of governance. Moreover, the evident urgency of this problem will open up the discursive space for proposals and paradigm shifts which were rightly considered "unthinkable" (or "utopian") even a short while ago.

This opening up of the horizon of considerations in policy-making and institution-building is furthermore facilitated by two rather novel features of the configuration of political forces. First, after the end of the cold war and systemic confrontation, political elites of OECD countries are no longer confronted by organised militant mass movements and "revolutionary" demands which are perceived to threaten the very foundations of social order. With such perceived threats absent, elites may well be able to afford a wider scope of learning, experimentation, and more courageous innovation than would otherwise have been deemed permissible and safe.

Second, not only has the potential for institutional innovation shifted from mass politics to elite politics; it has also shifted from the radical fringe of elites to the centre. For as the universe of operative political doctrines held by elite segments themselves has evidently shrunk to a rather narrow range of left-liberal vs. conservative liberal approaches, the rich traditions of republican political liberalism (as opposed to economic market liberalism) may well be rediscovered as an intellectual source for a design (such as the one advocated in this paper) for a new equilibrium of citizen rights and economic resources.

NOTES

1. Except, that is, for those who believe in the possibility of transferring significant amounts of labour power from industrial production to personal social services with its allegedly consistently lower rates of productivity increases and greater immunity from international competitive pressure.

2. To be sure, shifts in the reverse direction – *i.e.* from self-service to purchased services – can and do also occur, particularly in the upper ranges of income; examples include the externalisation of child care and the preparation of food from the private household to kindergarten and restaurants.

3. For a technical discussion of the two opposite effects, see Mark E. Killingsworth, *Labour Supply*, Cambridge University Press, 1987.

4. It is tempting to speculate about the reasons for this basic asymmetry (three types of interest vs. just two types of bargaining tables), but this is not the place to do so. Suffice it to say that the idea (and practice) of what would amount to a "second order contract" specifying the number of employees with whom an employer must enter into ordinary labour contracts is entirely alien to the realities of capitalist societies – as much as would be a contract between the collectives of buyers and sellers in a particular commodity market that stipulates a specific rate of profit for a specific period. In other words, there are limits beyond which market contingencies cannot possibly be "contractualised away".

5. This is the option to which both the German and the Swedish governments have committed themselves by their respective pledges to reduce unemployment by 50 per cent by the year 2000.

6. When considering a worker for employment, employers will take account not only of wage costs but also of the expected marginal product, *i.e.* the contribution of the hired worker towards the enterprise's output. It is by no means certain that, given the need for flexibility and the surplus skills and adaptability of workers called for by such flexibility requirements, prospective employers would not consider the typical low-skill-low-wage worker an obstacle to – rather than a factor of – (efficient) production. Even if such managerial micro-aversion against cheap labour were to be dismissed as largely irrelevant, the macroeconomic aggregate results of employers' preference for "cheap" labour would lead to the economy developing along a path of "static" rather than "dynamic" efficiency, and correspondingly losing in competitiveness. Thus it is evident that macroeconomic as well as managerial considerations speak against a low-wage

strategy aimed at pushing as many workers as possible into the labour market. The result, at best affordable in low-export economies such as the United States, might well be not unemployment due to high wages, but unemployment due to lagging international competitiveness – arguably even less desirable.

7. One (as yet unexplored) policy variant would involve contracting the temporal supply of labour not on the basis of collective agreements but as the employee's individual option to reduce his or her working time at will and within broad limits. This would mean according employees the right to make successive decisions on the duration of time, as well as the point in time, of their labour input. Such decisions would presumably be made according to the individual employee's shifting preferences for work and leisure, which in turn are conditioned by family, health, educational commitments, civic activities – even the weather. Without extensive experimentation, however, it is hard to predict the extent to which such legally protected "time optionality" would affect the volume of the firm's demand for labour, or employees' supply of it.

8. On this subject see Richard Titmuss, *The Gift Relationship: From Human Blood to Social Policy*, Allen & Unwin, London, 1970.

9. One fact that has received little attention: all West German taxpayers, in view of the situation imposed by unification, are prepared – at least for a limited period – to pay income transfers to every one of the 16 million new citizens in the eastern *Länder* of the Federal Republic of Germany, which roughly approximates the highest per capita amount awarded under the country's federal student aid programme. In practice, this amounts to granting a "citizens' income", which of course is for the present still missing theoretical justification.

10. The "killer phrase" usually put forth to prohibit such thinking is "weakening of the work incentive". This is an entirely unimpressive argument, as it can be countered by the argument that the maintenance or strengthening of the work incentive only makes sense when there is in fact a corresponding opportunity for work, *i.e.* a job, available, and that firms and markets are the only conceivable institutional contexts in which the individuals' will to work can be revealed, tested, and further developed.

Annex

LIST OF PARTICIPANTS

CHAIRMAN

Mr. Donald J. JOHNSTON
Secretary-General of the OECD

PARTICIPANTS

Mr. Thomas ALEXANDER
Director for Education, Employment,
Labour and Social Affairs
OECD

Mr. Roberto CARNEIRO
President
Televisão Independente SA (TVI)
Former Minister of Education
Portugal

Mr. Jacques DELORS
President
International Commission for
Education in the 21st Century
Former President, European Commission
France

Mr. Frederik A. von DEWALL
General Manager and Chief Economist
ING Bank
The Netherlands

Mr. Robert GOEBBELS
Minister of Economy, Public Works
and Transport
Luxembourg

Ms. Sumiko IWAO
Professor for Social Psychology
Keio University
Japan

Mr. Peter KALANTZIS
Member of the Executive Committee
Alusuisse-Lonza Holding Ltd.
Switzerland

Mr. Robert Z. LAWRENCE
Professor of Economics
John F. Kennedy School of Government
Harvard University
United States

Mr. Henri LEPAGE
Délégué Général
Institut Euro 92
France

Mr. Santiago LEVY
Under Secretary of State for Public Finance
Ministry of Finance
Mexico

Mr. Ruud LUBBERS
Professor of Economics
University of Tilburg
Former Prime Minister
The Netherlands

Mr. Peter MEDGYESSY
Minister of Finance
Hungary

Mr. A.P.W. MELKERT
Minister of Social Affairs and Employment
The Netherlands

Mr. Wolfgang MICHALSKI
Director
Advisory Unit to the Secretary-General
OECD

Mr. Claus OFFE
Professor of Political Sociology
and Social Policy
Humboldt University of Berlin
Germany

Mr. Yoichi OKITA
Vice Minister
International Economic Affairs
Economic Planning Agency
Japan

Mr. Leif PAGROTSKY
Minister of State
The Prime Minister's Office
Sweden

Mr. Robert (Bob) RAE Q.C.
Senior Partner
Goodman Philips and Vineberg
Former Premier of Ontario
Canada

Mr. Kumiharu SHIGEHARA
Head of the Economics Department
OECD

Mr. Dennis J. SNOWER
Professor of Economics
Birkbeck College,
University of London
United Kingdom

Mr. Fernando SOLANA MORALES
Senator
Former Minister of Foreign Affairs
Mexico

Mr. Bernd STECHER
Executive Vice President
Siemens AG
Germany

Mr. Makoto TANIGUCHI
Deputy Secretary-General
OECD

Mr. Werner TEGTMEYER
Secretary of State
Federal Ministry for Employment
and Social Affairs
Germany

Mr. Heiko THIEME
Chairman
American Heritage Management
Corporation
United States

OECD SECRETARIAT

Mr. Barrie STEVENS
Deputy Head
Advisory Unit to the Secretary-General

Mr. Riel MILLER
Principal Administrator
Advisory Unit to the Secretary-General

Mr. Pierre-Alain SCHIEB
Principal Administrator
Advisory Unit to the Secretary-General

MAIN SALES OUTLETS OF OECD PUBLICATIONS
PRINCIPAUX POINTS DE VENTE DES PUBLICATIONS DE L'OCDE

AUSTRALIA – AUSTRALIE
D.A. Information Services
648 Whitehorse Road, P.O.B 163
Mitcham, Victoria 3132   Tel. (03) 9210.7777
Fax: (03) 9210.7788

AUSTRIA – AUTRICHE
Gerold & Co.
Graben 31
Wien I   Tel. (0222) 533.50.14
Fax: (0222) 512.47.31.29

BELGIUM – BELGIQUE
Jean De Lannoy
Avenue du Roi, Koningslaan 202
B-1060 Bruxelles Tel. (02) 538.51.69/538.08.41
Fax: (02) 538.08.41

CANADA
Renouf Publishing Company Ltd.
5369 Canotek Road
Unit 1
Ottawa, Ont. K1J 9J3   Tel. (613) 745.2665
Fax: (613) 745.7660

Stores:
71 1/2 Sparks Street
Ottawa, Ont. K1P 5R1   Tel. (613) 238.8985
Fax: (613) 238.6041

12 Adelaide Street West
Toronto, QN M5H 1L6   Tel. (416) 363.3171
Fax: (416) 363.5963

Les Éditions La Liberté Inc.
3020 Chemin Sainte-Foy
Sainte-Foy, PQ G1X 3V6 Tel. (418) 658.3763
Fax: (418) 658.3763

Federal Publications Inc.
165 University Avenue, Suite 701
Toronto, ON M5H 3B8   Tel. (416) 860.1611
Fax: (416) 860.1608

Les Publications Fédérales
1185 Université
Montréal, QC H3B 3A7   Tel. (514) 954.1633
Fax: (514) 954.1635

CHINA – CHINE
Book Dept., China Natinal Publiations
Import and Export Corporation (CNPIEC)
16 Gongti E. Road, Chaoyang District
Beijing 100020 Tel. (10) 6506-6688 Ext. 8402
(10) 6506-3101

CHINESE TAIPEI – TAIPEI CHINOIS
Good Faith Worldwide Int'l. Co. Ltd.
9th Floor, No. 118, Sec. 2
Chung Hsiao E. Road
Taipei   Tel. (02) 391.7396/391.7397
Fax: (02) 394.9176

CZECH REPUBLIC –
RÉPUBLIQUE TCHÈQUE
National Information Centre
NIS – prodejna
Konviktská 5
Praha 1 – 113 57   Tel. (02) 24.23.09.07
Tel. (02) 24.22.94.33
E-mail: nkposp@dec.niz.cz
Internet: http://www.nis.cz

DENMARK – DANEMARK
Munksgaard Book and Subscription Service
35, Nørre Søgade, P.O. Box 2148
DK-1016 København K   Tel. (33) 12.85.70
Fax: (33) 12.93.87

J. H. Schultz Information A/S,
Herstedvang 12,
DK – 2620 Albertslung   Tel. 43 63 23 00
Fax: 43 63 19 69
Internet: s-info@inet.uni-c.dk

EGYPT – ÉGYPTE
The Middle East Observer
41 Sherif Street
Cairo   Tel. (2) 392.6919
Fax: (2) 360.6804

FINLAND – FINLANDE
Akateeminen Kirjakauppa
Keskuskatu 1, P.O. Box 128
00100 Helsinki

Subscription Services/Agence d'abonnements :
P.O. Box 23
00100 Helsinki   Tel. (358) 9.121.4403
Fax: (358) 9.121.4450

*FRANCE
OECD/OCDE
Mail Orders/Commandes par correspondance :
2, rue André-Pascal
75775 Paris Cedex 16 Tel. 33 (0)1.45.24.82.00
Fax: 33 (0)1.49.10.42.76
Telex: 640048 OCDE
Internet: Compte.PUBSINQ@oecd.org

Orders via Minitel, France only/
Commandes par Minitel, France
exclusivement : 36 15 OCDE

OECD Bookshop/Librairie de l'OCDE :
33, rue Octave-Feuillet
75016 Paris   Tel. 33 (0)1.45.24.81.81
33 (0)1.45.24.81.67

Dawson
B.P. 40
91121 Palaiseau Cedex   Tel. 01.89.10.47.00
Fax: 01.64.54.83.26

Documentation Française
29, quai Voltaire
75007 Paris   Tel. 01.40.15.70.00

Economica
49, rue Héricart
75015 Paris   Tel. 01.45.78.12.92
Fax: 01.45.75.05.67

Gibert Jeune (Droit-Économie)
6, place Saint-Michel
75006 Paris   Tel. 01.43.25.91.19

Librairie du Commerce International
10, avenue d'Iéna
75016 Paris   Tel. 01.40.73.34.60

Librairie Dunod
Université Paris-Dauphine
Place du Maréchal-de-Lattre-de-Tassigny
75016 Paris   Tel. 01.44.05.40.13

Librairie Lavoisier
11, rue Lavoisier
75008 Paris   Tel. 01.42.65.39.95

Librairie des Sciences Politiques
30, rue Saint-Guillaume
75007 Paris   Tel. 01.45.48.36.02

P.U.F.
49, boulevard Saint-Michel
75005 Paris   Tel. 01.43.25.83.40

Librairie de l'Université
12a, rue Nazareth
13100 Aix-en-Provence   Tel. 04.42.26.18.08

Documentation Française
165, rue Garibaldi
69003 Lyon   Tel. 04.78.63.32.23

Librairie Decitre
29, place Bellecour
69002 Lyon   Tel. 04.72.40.54.54

Librairie Sauramps
Le Triangle
34967 Montpellier Cedex 2 Tel. 04.67.58.85.15
Fax: 04.67.58.27.36

A la Sorbonne Actual
23, rue de l'Hôtel-des-Postes
06000 Nice   Tel. 04.93.13.77.75
Fax: 04.93.80.75.69

GERMANY – ALLEMAGNE
OECD Bonn Centre
August-Bebel-Allee 6
D-53175 Bonn   Tel. (0228) 959.120
Fax: (0228) 959.12.17

GREECE – GRÈCE
Librairie Kauffmann
Stadiou 28
10564 Athens   Tel. (01) 32.55.321
Fax: (01) 32.30.320

HONG-KONG
Swindon Book Co. Ltd.
Astoria Bldg. 3F
34 Ashley Road, Tsimshatsui
Kowloon, Hong Kong   Tel. 2376.2062
Fax: 2376.0685

HUNGARY – HONGRIE
Euro Info Service
Margitsziget, Európa Ház
1138 Budapest   Tel. (1) 111.60.61
Fax: (1) 302.50.35
E-mail: euroinfo@mail.matav.hu
Internet: http://www.euroinfo.hu//index.html

ICELAND – ISLANDE
Mál og Menning
Laugavegi 18, Pósthólf 392
121 Reykjavik   Tel. (1) 552.4240
Fax: (1) 562.3523

INDIA – INDE
Oxford Book and Stationery Co.
Scindia House
New Delhi 110001   Tel. (11) 331.5896/5308
Fax: (11) 332.2639
E-mail: oxford.publ@axcess.net.in

17 Park Street
Calcutta 700016   Tel. 240832

INDONESIA – INDONÉSIE
Pdii-Lipi
P.O. Box 4298
Jakarta 12042   Tel. (21) 573.34.67
Fax: (21) 573.34.67

IRELAND – IRLANDE
Government Supplies Agency
Publications Section
4/5 Harcourt Road
Dublin 2   Tel. 661.31.11
Fax: 475.27.60

ISRAEL – ISRAËL
Praedicta
5 Shatner Street
P.O. Box 34030
Jerusalem 91430   Tel. (2) 652.84.90/1/2
Fax: (2) 652.84.93

R.O.Y. International
P.O. Box 13056
Tel Aviv 61130   Tel. (3) 546 1423
Fax: (3) 546 1442
E-mail: royil@netvision.net.il

Palestinian Authority/Middle East:
INDEX Information Services
P.O.B. 19502
Jerusalem   Tel. (2) 627.16.34
Fax: (2) 627.12.19

ITALY – ITALIE
Libreria Commissionaria Sansoni
Via Duca di Calabria, 1/1
50125 Firenze   Tel. (055) 64.54.15
Fax: (055) 64.12.57
E-mail: licosa@ftbcc.it

Via Bartolini 29
20155 Milano   Tel. (02) 36.50.83

Editrice e Libreria Herder
Piazza Montecitorio 120
00186 Roma   Tel. 679.46.28
Fax: 678.47.51

Libreria Hoepli
Via Hoepli 5
20121 Milano   Tel. (02) 86.54.46
                      Fax: (02) 805.28.86

Libreria Scientifica
Dott. Lucio de Biasio 'Aeiou'
Via Coronelli, 6
20146 Milano   Tel. (02) 48.95.45.52
                      Fax: (02) 48.95.45.48

JAPAN – JAPON
OECD Tokyo Centre
Landic Akasaka Building
2-3-4 Akasaka, Minato-ku
Tokyo 107   Tel. (81.3) 3586.2016
                      Fax: (81.3) 3584.7929

KOREA – CORÉE
Kyobo Book Centre Co. Ltd.
P.O. Box 1658, Kwang Hwa Moon
Seoul   Tel. 730.78.91
                      Fax: 735.00.30

MALAYSIA – MALAISIE
University of Malaya Bookshop
University of Malaya
P.O. Box 1127, Jalan Pantai Baru
59700 Kuala Lumpur
Malaysia   Tel. 756.5000/756.5425
                      Fax: 756.3246

MEXICO – MEXIQUE
OECD Mexico Centre
Edificio INFOTEC
Av. San Fernando no. 37
Col. Toriello Guerra
Tlalpan C.P. 14050
Mexico D.F.   Tel. (525) 528.10.38
                      Fax: (525) 606.13.07
E-mail: ocde@rtn.net.mx

NETHERLANDS – PAYS-BAS
SDU Uitgeverij Plantijnstraat
Externe Fondsen
Postbus 20014
2500 EA's-Gravenhage Tel. (070) 37.89.880
Voor bestellingen: Fax: (070) 34.75.778

Subscription Agency/Agence d'abonnements :
SWETS & ZEITLINGER BV
Heereweg 347B
P.O. Box 830
2160 SZ Lisse   Tel. 252.435.111
                      Fax: 252.415.888

**NEW ZEALAND –
NOUVELLE-ZÉLANDE**
GPLegislation Services
P.O. Box 12418
Thorndon, Wellington Tel. (04) 496.5655
                      Fax: (04) 496.5698

NORWAY – NORVÈGE
NIC INFO A/S
Ostensjoveien 18
P.O. Box 6512 Etterstad
0606 Oslo   Tel. (22) 97.45.00
                      Fax: (22) 97.45.45

PAKISTAN
Mirza Book Agency
65 Shahrah Quaid-E-Azam
Lahore 54000   Tel. (42) 735.36.01
                      Fax: (42) 576.37.14

PHILIPPINE – PHILIPPINES
International Booksource Center Inc.
Rm 179/920 Cityland 10 Condo Tower 2
HV dela Costa Ext cor Valero St.
Makati Metro Manila   Tel. (632) 817 9676
                      Fax: (632) 817 1741

POLAND – POLOGNE
Ars Polona
00-950 Warszawa
Krakowskie Prezdmiescie 7 Tel. (22) 264760
                      Fax: (22) 265334

PORTUGAL
Livraria Portugal
Rua do Carmo 70-74
Apart. 2681
1200 Lisboa   Tel. (01) 347.49.82/5
                      Fax: (01) 347.02.64

SINGAPORE – SINGAPOUR
Ashgate Publishing
Asia Pacific Pte. Ltd
Golden Wheel Building, 04-03
41, Kallang Pudding Road
Singapore 349316   Tel. 741.5166
                      Fax: 742.9356

SPAIN – ESPAGNE
Mundi-Prensa Libros S.A.
Castelló 37, Apartado 1223
Madrid 28001   Tel. (91) 431.33.99
                      Fax: (91) 575.39.98
E-mail: mundiprensa@tsai.es
Internet: http://www.mundiprensa.es

Mundi-Prensa Barcelona
Consell de Cent No. 391
08009 – Barcelona   Tel. (93) 488.34.92
                      Fax: (93) 487.76.59

Libreria de la Generalitat
Palau Moja
Rambla dels Estudis, 118
08002 – Barcelona
             (Suscripciones) Tel. (93) 318.80.12
             (Publicaciones) Tel. (93) 302.67.23
                      Fax: (93) 412.18.54

SRI LANKA
Centre for Policy Research
c/o Colombo Agencies Ltd.
No. 300-304, Galle Road
Colombo 3   Tel. (1) 574240, 573551-2
                      Fax: (1) 575394, 510711

SWEDEN – SUÈDE
CE Fritzes AB
S–106 47 Stockholm   Tel. (08) 690.90.90
                      Fax: (08) 20.50.21

For electronic publications only/
Publications électroniques seulement
STATISTICS SWEDEN
Informationsservice
S-115 81 Stockholm   Tel. 8 783 5066
                      Fax: 8 783 4045

Subscription Agency/Agence d'abonnements :
Wennergren-Williams Info AB
P.O. Box 1305
171 25 Solna   Tel. (08) 705.97.50
                      Fax: (08) 27.00.71

Liber distribution
Internatinal organizations
Fagerstagatan 21
S-163 52 Spanga

SWITZERLAND – SUISSE
Maditec S.A. (Books and Periodicals/Livres
et périodiques)
Chemin des Palettes 4
Case postale 266
1020 Renens VD 1   Tel. (021) 635.08.65
                      Fax: (021) 635.07.80

Librairie Payot S.A.
4, place Pépinet
CP 3212
1002 Lausanne   Tel. (021) 320.25.11
                      Fax: (021) 320.25.14

Librairie Unilivres
6, rue de Candolle
1205 Genève   Tel. (022) 320.26.23
                      Fax: (022) 329.73.18

Subscription Agency/Agence d'abonnements :
Dynapresse Marketing S.A.
38, avenue Vibert
1227 Carouge   Tel. (022) 308.08.70
                      Fax: (022) 308.07.99

See also – Voir aussi :
OECD Bonn Centre
August-Bebel-Allee 6
D-53175 Bonn (Germany) Tel. (0228) 959.120
                      Fax: (0228) 959.12.17

THAILAND – THAÏLANDE
Suksit Siam Co. Ltd.
113, 115 Fuang Nakhon Rd.
Opp. Wat Rajbopith
Bangkok 10200   Tel. (662) 225.9531/2
                      Fax: (662) 222.5188

**TRINIDAD & TOBAGO, CARIBBEAN
TRINITÉ-ET-TOBAGO, CARAÏBES**
Systematics Studies Limited
9 Watts Street
Curepe
Trinidad & Tobago, W.I. Tel. (1809) 645.3475
                      Fax: (1809) 662.5654
E-mail: tobe@trinidad.net

TUNISIA – TUNISIE
Grande Librairie Spécialisée
Fendri Ali
Avenue Haffouz Imm El-Intilaka
Bloc B 1 Sfax 3000   Tel. (216-4) 296 855
                      Fax: (216-4) 298.270

TURKEY – TURQUIE
Kültür Yayinlari Is-Türk Ltd.
Atatürk Bulvari No. 191/Kat 13
06684 Kavaklidere/Ankara
                      Tel. (312) 428.11.40 Ext. 2458
                      Fax : (312) 417.24.90

Dolmabahce Cad. No. 29
Besiktas/Istanbul   Tel. (212) 260 7188

UNITED KINGDOM – ROYAUME-UNI
The Stationery Office Ltd.
Postal orders only:
P.O. Box 276, London SW8 5DT
Gen. enquiries   Tel. (171) 873 0011
                      Fax: (171) 873 8463

The Stationery Office Ltd.
Postal orders only:
49 High Holborn, London WC1V 6HB
Branches at: Belfast, Birmingham, Bristol,
Edinburgh, Manchester

UNITED STATES – ÉTATS-UNIS
OECD Washington Center
2001 L Street N.W., Suite 650
Washington, D.C. 20036-4922
                      Tel. (202) 785.6323
                      Fax: (202) 785.0350
Internet: washcont@oecd.org

Subscriptions to OECD periodicals may also
be placed through main subscription agencies.

Les abonnements aux publications périodiques
de l'OCDE peuvent être souscrits auprès des
principales agences d'abonnement.

Orders and inquiries from countries where Dis-
tributors have not yet been appointed should be
sent to: OECD Publications, 2, rue André-Pascal, 75775 Paris Cedex 16, France.

Les commandes provenant de pays où l'OCDE
n'a pas encore désigné de distributeur peuvent
être adressées aux Éditions de l'OCDE, 2, rue
André-Pascal, 75775 Paris Cedex 16, France.

12-1996

OECD PUBLICATIONS, 2, rue André-Pascal, 75775 PARIS CEDEX 16
PRINTED IN FRANCE
(03 97 03 1 P) ISBN 92-64-15484-1 – No. 49405 1997